Smart Parent's Guide to Cybersecurity

Anand Shinde and Jessen Kurien

Published by DevOM Publishing, 2025.

Published by DevOM Publishing 2025

ISBN 978-1-916865-25-9

Dedication

"To every parent who carries the quiet weight of protecting their children every day—this book is for you and dedicated to you. May it help you with the right guidance, understanding, and confidence to shield your loved ones from the unseen dangers of the advancing modern digital world. Your everyday care, patience, and love are the strongest defenses your children will ever know, and may this work help you nurture their curiosity, growth, and safety in equal measure.

This book is also dedicated to the countless individuals and professionals who work tirelessly to make our digital world safer for everyone, some known & many unknown. May this book honor your dedication and may all who navigate the online realm do so with confidence, awareness, and the tools to protect themselves and those they care for.

With lots of love & gratitude,

Anand & Jessen"

Acknowledgements by Anand Shinde

"I want to begin by expressing my deepest gratitude to my incredible wife, Shilpa Shinde, and my wonderful daughter, Aarushi Shinde. It's hard to find words that truly capture how much your love, understanding, and unwavering belief in me have meant. Your constant emotional support, patience, and the countless sacrifices you both made throughout this journey have been my strength. Without you, this book would not have been possible. I am beyond fortunate to walk through life with you by my side.

I am incredibly grateful to my spiritual mentor, Shri Rahul Makhi Guruji, who has been guiding me on my spiritual journey. He is responsible for my spiritual, personal, and professional growth. Without his selfless and honest guidance, my progress would never have been possible.

A heartfelt thank you also goes to Rafael Pluta, Karolina Korowacka, Marcel Balazi, and Krzysztof Poznanski. Your encouragement, advice, and belief in my writing have been a source of constant motivation. Your support kept me going, especially when the path ahead seemed unclear. I truly appreciate each of you for being part of this journey.

I am also deeply thankful to Dr Deepak Shikarpur, whose thoughtful guidance and perspective helped me see things from new angles. And to my best friend Saeed Inamdar, your unwavering support and encouragement were vital to keeping me focused and driven. Your faith in my work meant the world to me.

Lastly, I want to express my sincere gratitude to the global cybersecurity community. Your dedication to making the digital world safer inspires me daily. This book is a small way for me to contribute to that effort, and I hope it serves as a token of appreciation for all the work you do to secure our digital future."

Acknowledgements by Jessen Kurien

"My heartfelt appreciation goes to my parents, my family, and close friends, who taught me the value of perseverance and making me realize that "Giving is true having" in life.

The completion of this book represents both a professional milestone and a personal journey shaped by the guidance, mentorship, and encouragement of many remarkable individuals. I am deeply grateful to all who have supported and influenced me throughout my work in cybersecurity.

I owe special gratitude to Santosh Kandala, who not only hired me into one of my earliest cybersecurity roles but also served as a mentor and role model. His leadership, deep analytical rigor and extensive expertise in cyber threat intelligence, threat analysis, and security research have profoundly shaped my approach to identifying, understanding, and mitigating emerging cyber threats. His trust, guidance, and unwavering belief in my potential provided the foundation for my professional growth. His mentorship continues to influence how I lead, learn, and contribute to this field.

I would also like to thank Leah Lease, whose mentorship has been a constant source of inspiration. Her guidance has not only strengthened my technical and interpersonal skills but also instilled a disciplined, research-driven mindset that has been invaluable throughout my career and the development of this book.

I am also thankful to my colleagues and peers across the cybersecurity community who shared insights, challenged ideas, and contributed to the evolution of the thoughts captured in these pages.

To all my mentors, colleagues, and supporters — your wisdom, patience, and belief in this work have been indispensable. This book is as much a reflection of your influence as it is of my own effort."

Preface

"Parenting in the digital age is both an incredible opportunity and an overwhelming challenge. The internet has transformed the way children learn, play, and communicate, offering them access to knowledge, creativity, and connection like never before. Yet, alongside these benefits come serious risks—cyberbullying, online predators, privacy breaches, and the addictive pull of screens. As technology evolves, so do the threats, leaving many parents feeling unprepared to protect their children from the hidden dangers of the digital world.

Smart Parent's Guide to Cybersecurity is designed to bridge this gap. This book is not about instilling fear but about empowering parents with the knowledge and confidence to guide their children toward safe and responsible digital habits. It provides actionable solutions tailored to real-world parenting challenges, from managing screen time to addressing cyberbullying and teaching kids about online privacy. More importantly, it underscores the need for open communication, trust, and emotional support—ensuring that children feel safe coming to their parents when they encounter trouble online.

Cybersecurity is not just about installing parental controls or monitoring internet usage; it's about educating and equipping children with the skills to make responsible digital choices. This guide offers expert insights, practical strategies, and real-life examples to help parents navigate these complex issues with clarity and confidence. Whether you are introducing your child to the internet for the first time or dealing with more advanced online risks, this book serves as a roadmap to creating a secure and enriching digital environment for your family.

By reading this guide, you are taking the first step toward raising a digitally aware and resilient child. You are not alone on this journey. Together, we can prepare the next generation to be confident, responsible digital citizens in an ever-changing online world."

About the Author

"Anand Shinde is a renowned, seasoned Cybersecurity expert, mentor, and author with a wealth of experience in safeguarding digital ecosystems, as a certified professional with credentials from global leaders like Microsoft, Cisco, Amazon, ISACA and the International Society of Automation. Anand has worked on complex cybersecurity projects across India, Poland, Ireland, and the United States. His international career has equipped him with diverse perspectives and practical insights to address intricate cybersecurity challenges effectively.

In addition to his consulting work, Anand is deeply committed to education and mentorship. Since 2015, he has been serving as a student mentor and career counsellor for prestigious institutions, including Novel Group of Institutes and MIT ADT University, guiding aspiring professionals toward successful careers in cybersecurity. His role as a mentor for the International Society of Automation reflects his dedication to fostering talent in the ever-evolving cyber landscape.

Anand has also contributed to the field of cybersecurity and artificial intelligence with an innovative patent application, underscoring his commitment to advancing the industry. His contributions extend to raising cyber awareness through blogs and campaigns that promote best practices for digital strength.

For anyone aspiring to build a career in cybersecurity, Anand invites you to connect through AnandShinde.com, where he continues to empower individuals and organizations to thrive in the digital age."

About the Author

"With over 18 years of experience in cybersecurity, Jessen Kurien has dedicated his professional life to protecting organizations from the world's most sophisticated digital threats. With a career spanning top industry players like Microsoft, he has led global initiatives in Cyber Security Operations, Threat Intelligence, Threat Detection, Incident Response, Cloud Security, Risk Management & AI-driven Cyber defense.

After spending close to 15 years at Microsoft, today he works as a consultant, helping organizations tackle complex AI and cybersecurity challenges and implement effective automated solutions. His work combines strategic leadership with hands-on technical expertise, supporting clients in optimizing security operations and driving innovation bridging both the technical and human aspects of security. He has led development of various advanced Machine Learning and Artificial Intelligence based cyber threat detections enhancing the organization's defenses through sophisticated threat analysis and detection strategies, helping prevent potential breaches as well as the financial and operational consequences they would entail. Jessen was a member of the founding Microsoft Threat Intelligence Center (MSTIC) team,

contributed to defending against nation-state attacks, ransomware campaigns, and supply-chain breaches that shaped the global cybersecurity landscape. He has led global SOC teams and has authored numerous blogs on critical cybersecurity topics, delivering impactful guidance that has proven valuable to cybersecurity professionals and everyday users.

Jessen has previously held several industry-recognized certifications including Certified Ethical Hacker (CEH), CCNA CyberOps, CWNA, and ISO 27001-certified professional demonstrating a strong grounding in security governance, operations, and threat response. His expertise in 8 different SIEM (Security Information and Event Management) solutions and advanced computer forensic investigation training thwarted various advanced cyberattacks and mitigated large-scale data breaches helping organizations safeguard critical systems and sensitive information. Jessen always believed that true cybersecurity extends beyond firewalls and systems — it begins at home. His extensive experience leading red-team exercises, risk assessments, and SOC leadership has given him a deep appreciation for one simple truth: the most vulnerable systems are not machines, but unprepared minds.

When he's not at work, he loves dedicating his time to building and supporting the local community. He founded and leads a community initiative that now unites over 30,000 residents — a remarkable citywide network that has helped families rebuild after hardship, supported mothers in need, reunited lost pets with their owners, clothed and fed the homeless, raised awareness of local issues, and created safe spaces for mental health support. This thriving movement has inspired neighbors to lift one another through acts of kindness. In addition, he mentors young people, coaches high school students on career development, and gives talks on cybersecurity, demonstrating that true leadership blends vision with compassion in action.

For Jessen, this book is not just a guide — it's a commitment to every parent who feels unprepared to protect their child online. It distills two decades of professional expertise into practical, relatable insights that any caregiver can apply. From understanding cyberbullying and phishing to nurturing digital discipline, Jessen brings both the precision of a cyber security expert and compassion to every parent.

That realization inspired him, together with Mr. Anand Shinde, to write "Smart Parent's Guide to Cybersecurity." Both cybersecurity professionals have seen firsthand how today's digital world surrounds children with opportunity and risk in equal measures.

He firmly believes that cybersecurity begins with conversation — between parents and children, between technology and trust. Through this book, Jessen and Anand invite parents everywhere to join that conversation and take an active role in shaping a safer, smarter digital future for their families.

For questions on cybersecurity, technology strategy, or career coaching, Jessen can be reached directly at https://www.jessenkurien.com."

Welcome

"Welcome to Smart Parent's Guide to Cybersecurity—your essential companion in navigating the challenges and opportunities of raising children in the digital age. If you've ever felt overwhelmed by the complexities of the online world or unsure about how to protect your child from cyber risks, you're not alone. This book is here to provide you with clarity, confidence, and practical strategies to create a safe and positive digital experience for your family.

The internet is an incredible tool for learning, creativity, and connection, but it also presents real dangers, from cyberbullying and online predators to privacy breaches and screen addiction. As parents, our role is not to shelter our children from technology but to equip them with the skills and knowledge to navigate it wisely. This guide is designed to help you do just that—by fostering open communication, building trust, and implementing effective security measures tailored to your family's needs.

Throughout this book, you'll find expert advice, real-world examples, and actionable solutions that address modern parenting concerns. Whether you're managing screen time, teaching responsible social media habits, or handling a cybersecurity incident, this book will serve as a valuable resource every step of the way.

We believe that digital parenting is not about fear, but about empowerment. By understanding the risks and learning how to mitigate them, you can help your child become a confident and responsible digital citizen. So, take a deep breath—you're not alone on this journey. Together, we can create a secure, balanced, and enriching online environment for our children.

Let's get started!"

Chapter 1: The Digital Age and Our Kids

The digital age powered by AI today has totally transformed the way we live, work, and play, bringing with it countless opportunities and challenges. One of the most significant changes is the increasing presence of the internet in our children's lives. From online learning and social media to gaming and entertainment, the internet has become an integral part of their daily routines.

In today's world, children are introduced to digital devices at a very young age. They use tablets and smartphones for educational purposes, connect with friends through social media, and explore a vast array of online games and videos. This constant connectivity offers numerous benefits, such as access to information, educational resources, and social interactions that were previously unimaginable.

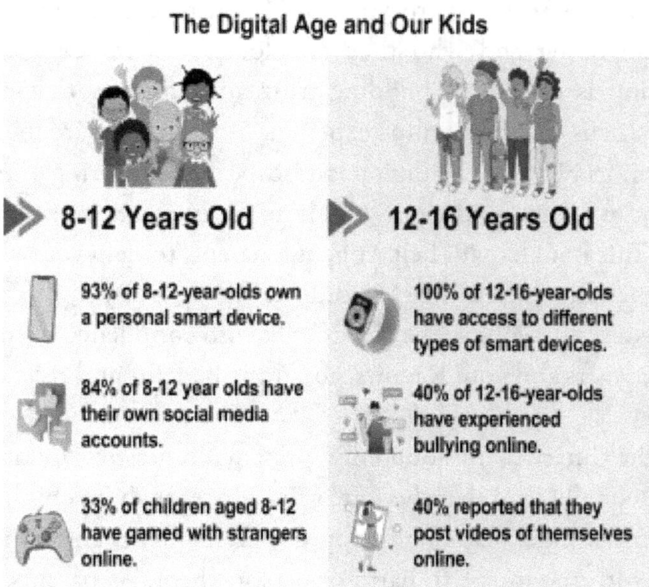

A recent survey highlights just how prevalent internet usage has become among children. For example, 93% of 8-12-year-olds own a personal smart device, and 100% of 12-16-year-olds have access to different types of smart devices. This widespread ownership underscores the importance of understanding how our children are engaging with the digital world.

Children not only own these devices but are also active on social media and instant messaging platforms. Around 84% of 8-12-year-olds have their own social media accounts, with YouTube, WhatsApp, TikTok, and Snapchat being the most popular. This trend continues with older children, making it clear that social media is a significant part of their lives.

However, this increased internet usage also brings potential risks that parents need to be aware of. Cyberbullying, exposure to inappropriate content, and online predators are just a few of the dangers that our children may encounter. For instance, 40% of 12-16-year-olds have experienced bullying online, with a higher percentage of girls reporting such incidents compared to boys. Additionally, 33% of children aged 8-12 have gamed with strangers online, highlighting another area of concern.

As parents, it is crucial to understand these risks and take proactive steps to protect our children in the digital world. The best online safety strategy, regardless of age, is to talk with your child and to engage with them about what they are doing and who they are doing it with. Open and regular communication is critical to building trust and ensuring that children feel comfortable discussing their online experiences with their parents.

By becoming aware of the digital landscape and educating ourselves about cybersecurity, we can guide our children to use the internet safely and responsibly. This booklet will help you, as a parent, to help your children have a positive experience when they are online. It will give you information and advice and, as a result, you will be able to talk with confidence to your children, including teenagers and young adults, about the benefits and risks they need to be aware of.

While the internet undoubtedly presents fantastic opportunities for children, it is equally clear that there are valid concerns about children spending too much time online, accessing inappropriate content, and communicating with people with the intent to harm or exploit them. As parents, our natural desire is to keep our children safe. This book provides practical advice and resources to help you navigate these challenges.

By following the guidance provided here, you will be better equipped to protect your children and ensure they have a positive, enriching experience in the digital world. Together, we can help our children navigate the complexities of the digital age with confidence and security.

1.1 The Importance of Internet Access for Kids

In our modern world, internet connection is a crucial component of everyday life, especially for our children. It is no longer a luxury but rather a need, much like electricity or running water. The internet is important in many parts of children's lives, providing countless benefits that can help them study, develop socially, and feel better overall.

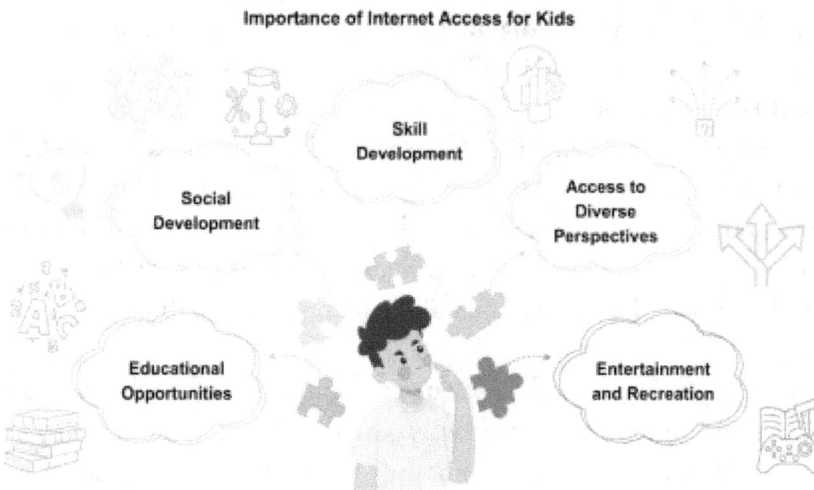

Educational Opportunities

One significant benefit of an internet connection is the vast number of educational resources available online. Children have access to a wide range of information and learning resources that supplement their formal education. Websites, online courses, and educational applications provide dynamic and exciting material, making learning enjoyable and effective. Subjects that may be difficult in a typical classroom environment can be studied at the child's speed, resulting in a more individualized learning experience.

For example, Khan Academy, National Geographic Kids, and instructional YouTube channels offer videos, tutorials, and exercises on a variety of topics.

This type of access fosters children's love of learning and stimulates curiosity about their surroundings.

Social Development

Internet connectivity is also essential for children's social development. Social media platforms, messaging applications, and online forums enable children to maintain contact with friends and family, mainly when actual interactions are not feasible. These platforms allow students to share their experiences, work on projects, and encourage one another.

Furthermore, online groups might be beneficial for youngsters who feel alone or are unable to establish friends in their surrounding area. They may connect with like-minded individuals and form supportive connections, which can dramatically improve their self-esteem and social skills.

Skill Development

The internet is an effective instrument for learning a variety of skills required for the future. Children may pursue a variety of hobbies online, from fundamental computer literacy to more advanced capabilities such as coding, graphic design, and digital marketing. Many platforms provide free or low-cost classes that teach these essential skills and prepare children for the digital economy.

For example, websites like Code.org and Scratch teach youngsters to program in a fun and interactive way, whereas Canva allows kids to explore with visual design. These qualities not only benefit future employment but also promote creativity and problem-solving ability.

Access to Diverse Perspectives

The internet connects children to a worldwide community, allowing them to learn about many cultures, opinions, and ideas. This exposure is critical for cultivating empathy, comprehension, and a larger perspective. Children can take part in virtual exchange programs, view films, and have discussions with classmates from all backgrounds.

Understanding and valuing variety allows youngsters to become more open-minded and polite people. This global awareness is a vital part of their personal development and allows children to navigate an increasingly linked world.

Entertainment and Recreation

Beyond education and social connection, the internet offers an abundance of recreational activities alternatives. Streaming services, internet games, and virtual reality experiences allow youngsters to relax and have fun. These activities can also spark creativity and inspiration in children, encouraging them to pursue new hobbies and interests.

However, parents must help their children balance entertainment with other activities and ensure that screen time is adequately handled.

In today's digital world, children's growth and development relies heavily on internet connectivity. It brings up a variety of possibilities, ranging from educational resources and skill development to social relationships and cultural awareness. As parents, we must guarantee that our children use the internet securely and responsibly, maximizing its advantages while limiting possible hazards. By being aware and active, we can help our children use the internet to become well-rounded, intelligent, and supportive persons.

1.2 Educational Benefits of the Internet

The internet has transformed education by giving students incomparable access to previously unthinkable knowledge and learning tools. For kids, the digital revolution has several educational benefits that can improve academic achievement, promote lifelong learning, and cultivate critical thinking abilities. Here are some significant educational benefits of the Internet for children:

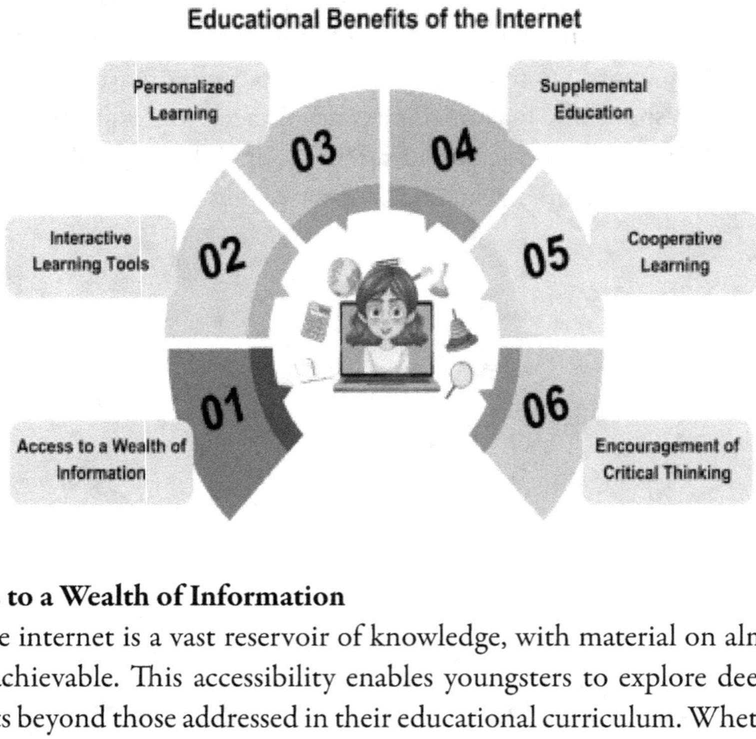

Access to a Wealth of Information

The internet is a vast reservoir of knowledge, with material on almost any topic achievable. This accessibility enables youngsters to explore deeply into subjects beyond those addressed in their educational curriculum. Whether they are studying for a school assignment, seeking data for a scientific experiment, or simply fulfilling their curiosity, the internet gives them fast access to reliable data from credible sources.

Websites such as Wikipedia, educational portals, and digital libraries provide a wealth of materials that may help a youngster learn a variety of subjects. This large collection of knowledge helps youngsters develop research skills and promotes their becoming self-sufficient learners.

Interactive Learning Tools

One of the internet's major benefits is the availability of interactive learning resources. These technologies make teaching more interesting and enjoyable, encouraging youngsters to learn more successfully. Online quizzes, instructional games, and interactive simulations enable children to practice and apply what they have learned in a hands-on setting.

For example, BrainPOP and ABCmouse provide interactive lessons and activities geared to various age groups and learning styles. These platforms employ animations, games, and quizzes to teach ideas in an engaging and instructive manner.

Personalized Learning

The internet allows tailored learning experiences, allowing students to study at their speed and based on their interests. Unlike traditional classrooms, where the speed of instruction is frequently consistent, online materials may be customized to individual requirements. Children can repeat complex themes, jump forward if they understand concepts quickly, and investigate issues that attract their interest.

Khan Academy and Coursera provide tailored learning paths, including video courses, practice tasks, and progress tracking. This approach helps youngsters lay a solid foundation in various areas and gain a more profound knowledge of the material.

Supplemental Education

The Internet is a beautiful addition to conventional schooling. It offers additional tools and assistance to help youngsters succeed academically. Online tutoring programs, homework help websites, and educational forums provide support outside of school hours, ensuring that youngsters have the resources they need to achieve.

For example, companies such as Chegg and Tutor.com match students with tutors who can assist them with specific topics or tasks. These platforms give customized attention and advice to youngsters, reinforcing what they learn in school and helping them overcome academic problems.

Cooperative Learning

The Internet promotes collaborative learning by linking students with their classmates and instructors worldwide. Online forums, study groups, and collaborative projects enable students to collaborate, exchange ideas, and learn from one another. This collaborative setting encourages students to develop cooperation and communication skills, both of which are critical for success in today's society.

Educational platforms such as Google Classroom and Edmodo facilitate collaboration. These platforms offer capabilities for group projects, debates, and feedback. These systems allow students to participate in real-time, independent of physical location, resulting in a dynamic and engaging learning experience.

Encouragement of Critical Thinking

The internet promotes critical thinking by exposing youngsters to a variety of viewpoints and facts. When youngsters conduct internet research, they learn to evaluate sources, identify reputable material, and understand various points of view. These abilities are essential for cultivating a critical attitude and making sound judgments.

Children learn to think critically about information by engaging in online discussions, reading varied articles, and participating in discussion forums. This critical thinking capacity is a vital life skill that will help them succeed in school and beyond.

The Internet offers several educational benefits for youngsters. The internet has the potential to alter education by providing access to a multitude of knowledge and interactive learning tools, as well as individualized and collaborative learning opportunities. As parents, we must lead our children in using the internet efficiently, ensuring that they make full use of these educational possibilities while being secure online. By embracing the internet's educational benefits, we may help our children gain the information, skills, and critical thinking abilities required to flourish in the age of digital technology.

1.3 Overall Development through Digital Interaction

Digital contact has become a vital part of children's lives, with a variety of sound effects on their general development. Beyond academic learning, the internet and digital technology play an essential role in promoting social, emotional, and cognitive development. Here are some significant ways in which digital engagement adds to children's overall development:

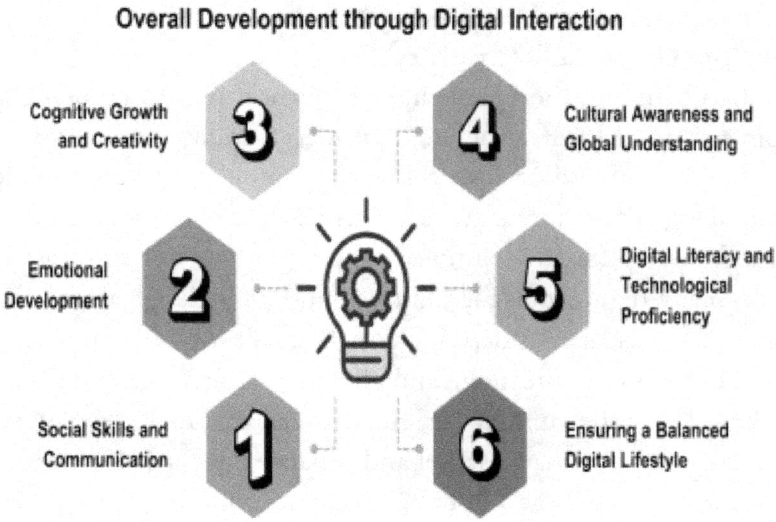

Social Skills and Communication

Digital platforms give youngsters countless chances to improve their social skills and communication. Children may engage with friends, family members, and others from all over the world using social media, messaging applications, and online forums. These encounters teach students how to speak effectively, convey their thoughts and emotions, and appreciate different viewpoints.

For example, participation in group conversations or collaborative projects online teaches kids how to work in groups, share duties, and settle problems. These experiences are beneficial in developing strong interpersonal skills, which are necessary for both their personal and professional life.

Emotional Development

The internet provides a variety of materials to help children's emotional development. Online forums and support groups allow youngsters to share their experiences, seek guidance, and find encouragement. This sense of belonging and support is beneficial for youngsters who may feel lonely or suffer difficulties in their daily lives.

Furthermore, instructional information on emotional intelligence, such as films and articles about empathy, resilience, and coping skills, can help youngsters better understand and control their emotions. Apps and websites that encourage mindfulness and mental health awareness improve their emotional well-being.

Cognitive Growth and Creativity

Children benefit from digital engagement because it promotes cognitive development and creativity. The internet offers a wide range of instructional games, puzzles, and activities that test their problem-solving abilities and critical thinking. These interactive activities teach youngsters to think outside the box and develop creative solutions.

Additionally, digital tools for painting, music, and design allow youngsters to express their creative side. Apps such as Canva for graphic design, GarageBand for music creation, and different digital sketching platforms provide limitless opportunities for creative expression. By exploring these instruments, youngsters may discover and enhance their artistic ability.

Cultural Awareness and Global Understanding

The internet introduces children to a worldwide society, exposing them to many cultures, customs, and ways of life. Through internet interactions and material, children may learn about many cultures, celebrate diversity, and acquire a more global perspective. This cultural knowledge cultivates empathy, tolerance, and respect for others.

Children, for example, may explore and appreciate the richness of global variety through virtual exchange programs, international pen pal projects, and cultural films. These encounters shape them into more open-minded and culturally aware persons.

Digital Literacy and Technological Proficiency

In today's digital world, being technologically literate is an essential ability. Digital contact helps youngsters become proficient with technology, preparing them for the future job market and everyday life. They learn how to explore the internet, operate software apps, and comprehend the fundamentals of online security and privacy.

Educational platforms and coding websites, such as Code.org and Scratch, introduce kids to the world of programming and technology. These abilities are useful not only for future employment but also for understanding and ethically participating in the digital world.

Ensuring a Balanced Digital Lifestyle

While digital connections have various advantages, it is critical to balance screen time with offline activity. Encouraging children to engage in physical activities, hobbies, and face-to-face contact is critical to their general development. Parents may create boundaries and instil appropriate screen time habits to promote a well-rounded lifestyle.

Digital interactions significantly influence children's entire development. It helps them improve their social skills, emotional well-being, cognitive development, creativity, cultural awareness, and digital literacy. As parents, we must help our children navigate the digital world. Encouraging a balanced approach to digital contact helps our children realize the benefits of technology while also developing them into well-rounded, knowledgeable, and sympathetic persons. We can build a healthy digital environment that promotes our children's overall development by practicing attentive and involved parenting.

1.4 Balancing Online and Offline Activities

In today's digital age, kids are more pulled to the attraction of the internet, which offers a wide range of entertainment, educational materials, and social contacts. While these online activities have tremendous advantages, it is also critical to ensure that children maintain a good balance between their online and offline lives. Achieving this balance is critical to their general health, growth, and enjoyment.

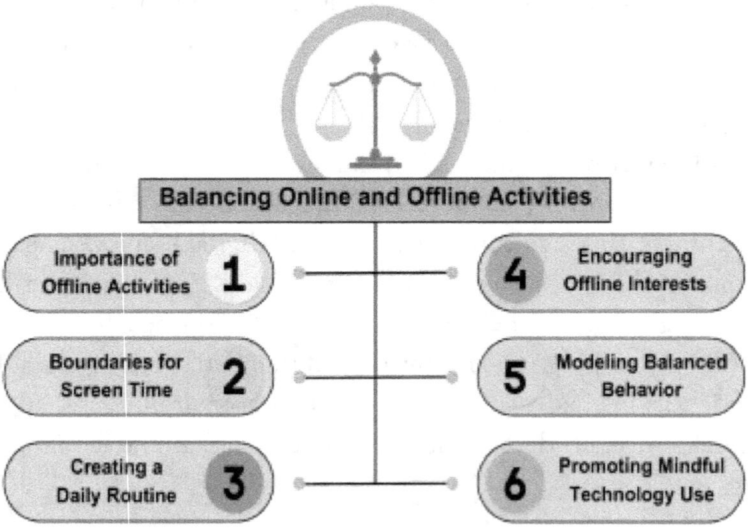

Importance of Offline Activities

Offline activities are extremely important for a child's growth. They offer chances for physical activity, social connection, and artistic expression, all of which are necessary for a well-rounded upbringing. Sports, outdoor activities, hobbies such as reading or painting, and spending quality time with family and friends all help kids develop physical, emotional, and social qualities that are not often promoted online.

Physical activities, for example, are essential for overall health. Regular exercise helps prevent obesity, strengthens the heart and muscles, and enhances coordination and motor abilities. Furthermore, outdoor play helps kids explore their surroundings, stimulating their creativity and imagination.

Boundaries for Screen Time

One of the most efficient strategies for combining online and offline activities is to establish clear screen time limits. Parents can set guidelines to limit how much time their children spend on technology each day. These restrictions should be sensible and include the child's age, requirements, and daily routine.

For example, the American Academy of Pediatrics advises no more than one hour of screen usage per day for children aged two to five, with comparable restrictions for older kids and teenagers. Setting these boundaries allows parents to ensure that their children have enough time for offline activities while avoiding the negative impacts of excessive screen time, such as eye strain, sleep disruptions, and decreased physical activity.

Creating a Daily Routine

Creating a daily routine that involves both online and offline activities might help kids manage their time more successfully. Parents may make a balanced timetable that includes defined hours for academics, online learning, and recreational screen time, as well as physical activity, hobbies, and family interactions.

For example, a daily schedule may include morning exercise, online lessons throughout the school day, an afternoon outdoor activity or hobby, and minimal screen time in the evening. Following a set schedule allows youngsters to develop effective time management skills and learn the need to balance many elements of their lives.

Encouraging Offline Interests

Parents can encourage their children to pursue offline activities that they are enthusiastic about. Sports, music, arts and crafts, reading, and gardening are all examples of non-screen hobbies and pastimes that may be extremely enjoyable and rewarding.

Giving children the resources and experiences they need to follow their interests is critical. This might include enrolling them in sports teams, painting classes, or music lessons, as well as providing them with the required materials and equipment. Celebrating their successes in these areas encourages them to pursue their offline interests.

Modeling Balanced Behavior

Children frequently replicate their parents' conduct, so parents must model a balanced attitude to both online and offline activities. Displaying healthy screen habits, such as putting aside digital devices during family meals or engaging in regular physical activity, can establish a good example for kids to look up to.

Parents may also engage in offline activities with their children, such as playing sports, taking walks, or working on creative projects. These shared experiences not only build family relationships but also highlight the importance of balancing screen time with other activities.

Promoting Mindful Technology Use

Teaching children to use technology responsibly is another critical component of balancing online and offline activity. Mindful technology usage is being aware of how much time one spends online, understanding the purpose of digital activities, and making deliberate decisions about when and how to use digital devices.

Parents should encourage mindful usage by emphasizing the value of taking breaks, avoid multitasking with numerous devices, and being picky about what information they consume. Encouraging children to engage in instructive and stimulating digital activities, rather than passive consumption, can help them develop a better connection with technology.

Children's general growth and well-being require a balance of online and outside activities. Parents can assist their children in navigating the digital world while maintaining a healthy and meaningful offline existence by setting screen time limits, developing daily routines, encouraging offline hobbies, modelling balanced conduct, and advocating mindful technology use. This balance allows kids to get the benefits of the internet while simultaneously enjoying the joys and advantages of offline activities.

1.5 Parental Challenges in the Digital World for Kids

In today's fast-paced digital age, parental involvement in their children's online activities has never been more crucial. However, many parents find themselves struggling to keep up with the rapidly changing digital landscape. The Internet, with its vast range of information, opportunities, and potential dangers, has become an integral part of children's lives. Yet, parents often feel unprepared to monitor or manage their children's digital activities effectively.

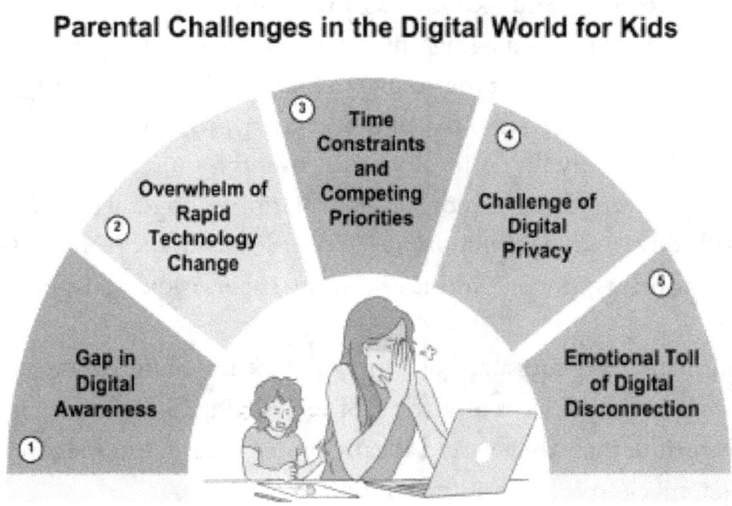

The Gap in Digital Awareness

Many parents today grew up without the Internet, social media, or smartphones. As a result, they may need more technical knowledge to understand the digital environments their children are navigating daily entirely. This knowledge gap can make it challenging for parents to keep pace with the platforms, apps, and games that captivate their children's attention.

For instance, while children may be fluent in the latest social media trends, many parents need to familiarize themselves with how these platforms work, what kind of content their children are exposed to, or who they are interacting with online. This lack of digital fluency creates a significant barrier to effective parental involvement and oversight.

The Overwhelm of Rapid Technological Change

The digital world is constantly evolving, with new apps, games, and social media platforms emerging constantly. For parents, keeping up with these changes can be overwhelming. Even if a parent becomes familiar with a particular platform, it may quickly be replaced by something new, leaving them once again in the dark.

This rapid pace of change can leave parents feeling powerless or out of touch, unsure of where to start or how to keep up. It can also lead to a sense of resignation, where parents might choose to disengage rather than continually struggle to stay informed about their children's online activities.

Time Constraints and Competing Priorities

Many parents are managing multiple responsibilities, including work, household duties, and caring for younger children. These competing demands can make it challenging to find the time and energy to monitor their children's online activities closely. In an ideal world, parents would have the time to sit down with their children, explore digital platforms together, and engage in meaningful conversations about online safety. However, the reality is that many parents are too busy to provide the level of supervision and guidance they would like.

Additionally, the pressures of work and other obligations can lead to parents using digital devices as a form of babysitting, allowing their children more screen time than they would ideally prefer. This could heighten the gap between parents and their children's online lives.

The Challenge of Digital Privacy

Another significant challenge is the issue of digital privacy. As children grow older, they often become more protective of their online spaces, seeking independence and privacy from their parents. This can create difficulty for parents, who want to respect their children's privacy but also feel responsible for ensuring their safety online.

In many cases, parents may be unaware of the extent of their children's online activities because these activities are conducted in private, through personal devices such as smartphones or tablets. This lack of visibility can make it difficult for parents to identify potential risks or intervene when necessary.

The Emotional Toll of Digital Disconnection

For some parents, the digital divide between themselves and their children can lead to feelings of guilt, frustration, or shortcomings. They may worry that they are failing to protect their children from online dangers or that they are missing out on an essential aspect of their children's lives. The societal expectation that parents should be fully engaged in all aspects of their children's upbringing, including their digital lives, can increase this emotional toll.

Parents may also feel isolated as they need more support and guidance to understand the complexities of the digital world. This can lead to a sense of helplessness, where parents may feel that they are unable to provide the necessary guidance and protection for their children in the online space.

Many parents face significant challenges and obstacles when it comes to being involved in their children's digital lives. A lack of digital fluency, the overwhelming pace of technological change, time constraints, and the need to respect their children's privacy all contribute to the difficulty parents face in monitoring and guiding their children's online activities. Moreover, the emotional burden of feeling disconnected from this important aspect of their children's lives can further complicate their efforts.

As we move forward in this book, the focus will shift to addressing these challenges and providing practical advice on how parents can become more involved in their children's digital lives. But first, it is essential to acknowledge the reality of the situation many parents find themselves in—a reality where, despite their best intentions, they may feel unprepared and overwhelmed by the demands of the digital world.

Chapter 2: Understanding Kids Online Activities

As the digital world develops, so does the variety of online activities that our children participate in. The Internet provides an engaging atmosphere in which children can study, socialize, play, and create. Understanding these many activities is critical for parents seeking to help and safeguard their children in this ever-changing world.

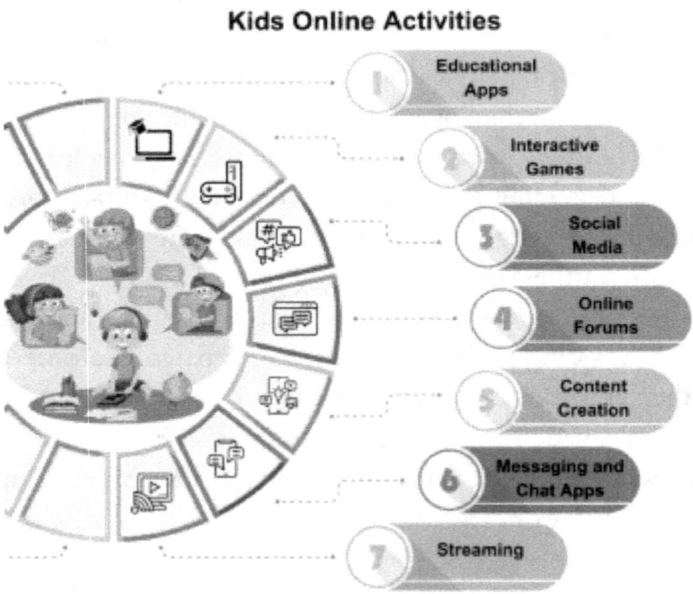

Today's kids are digital natives, meaning they grew up with technology easily integrated into their daily lives. From an early age, students connect with technological devices for a variety of purposes, including instructional apps and interactive games, as well as viewing films and using social media. As kids become older, their online behaviors become more complicated and diverse, reflecting their changing interests and developmental stage.

The Internet is frequently used by younger children for both excitement and education. Educational games and movies may help them improve their intellectual and physical abilities, and storytelling applications and animated programs can spark their imagination. However, even at this young age, children are vulnerable to dangers such as unsuitable information and online predators. As a result, parental engagement and supervision are critical in shaping their children's early digital experiences.

As kids go into their pre-teen and teenage stages, their internet activities change dramatically. Social media platforms, messaging applications, and online forums play an increasingly important role in their social relationships. They utilize these platforms to communicate with their friends, discuss their lives, and discover their identities. Online gaming also plays an important role in encouraging cooperation, competitiveness, and creative expression. However, these platforms also provide risks such as cyberbullying, privacy problems, and the temptation to adhere to identities on the Internet.

The development of user-generated material has increased the variety of internet activities for children. Platforms such as YouTube, TikTok, and Instagram enable kids to make and share their videos, music, and art, promoting creativity and personal expression. While this may be extremely powerful, it also requires a thorough awareness of digital etiquette, privacy settings, and the possibility of online criticism.

To successfully navigate this complicated digital terrain, parents must remain up to date on the newest trends and technology that influence their children's online experiences. This necessitates not just recognizing the sorts of activities that appeal to children but also being aware of the potential dangers and advantages connected with each activity. By being active and knowledgeable, parents can help their children make safe and informed online decisions.

In this chapter, we will examine the most prevalent online activities for different age groups, the trends that influence children's internet usage, and a statistical summary of how children interact with technology. We will also discuss the function of social media, the effects of online gaming, and the importance of content production in children's lives. This comprehensive examination will provide parents with the understanding and assets they need to create a healthy and safe digital environment for their children.

Understanding children's online behaviors requires more than just monitoring their screen time; it also includes interacting with them, learning about their interests, and leading them toward healthy and enjoyable digital experiences. By doing so, parents can help their children navigate the digital world with confidence, curiosity, and a strong feeling of security.

2.1 Common Online Activities for Different Age Groups

Understanding the usual internet activities that children participate in at various stages of development is critical for parents. This information is helpful in directing their digital experiences and guaranteeing their safety. Here are some everyday internet activities for different age groups:

A) Ages 3-5: Early Childhood

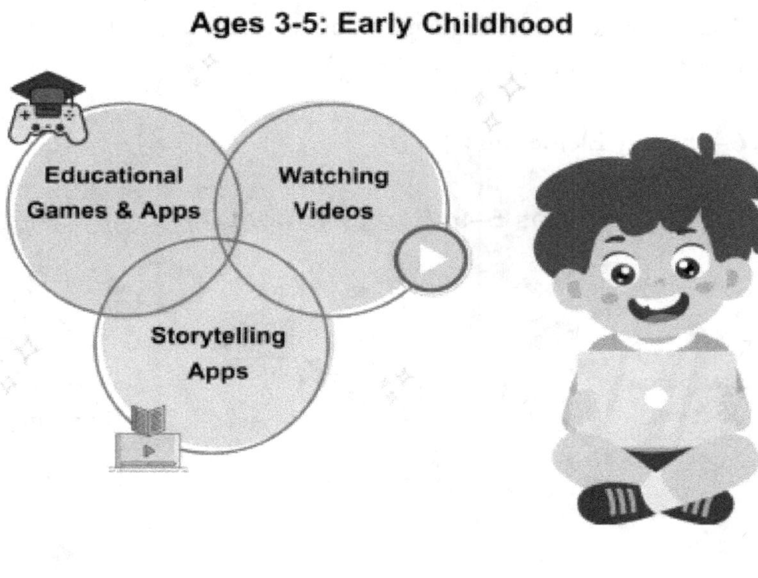

1) Educational Games & Apps

- Young children frequently use tablets and smartphones to play educational games that help them develop their motor and intellectual skills. Apps such as ABCmouse and Khan Academy Kids provide interactive reading, mathematics, and other educational opportunities.
- These games are intended to be fun and instructive, allowing youngsters to learn through playing.

2) Watching Videos

- Platforms such as YouTube Kids provide a wide range of age-appropriate content. Children of this age love watching cartoons, instructional shows, and nursery rhymes.
- Parents can set up playlists with authorized content to guarantee a safe watching experience.

3) Storytelling Apps

- Epic! and Toca Boca are two storytelling applications that use interactive and animated stories to fascinate young audiences.
- These applications frequently contain reading-aloud options and interactive components that bring books to life.

B) Ages 6–9: Early Elementary

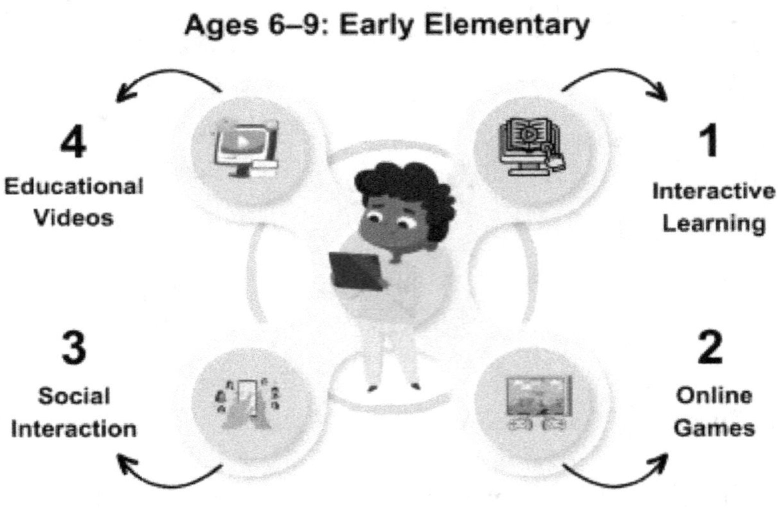

1) Interactive Learning

- Children begin to utilize the Internet for interactive educational activities. Websites such as National Geographic Kids and BrainPOP provide instructional movies, quizzes, and games to make learning enjoyable.

- These platforms provide a diverse range of topics, including science, history, and geography.

2) Online Games

- Games like Minecraft and Roblox are popular among those in this age group. These games not only entertain but also promote creativity and problem-solving abilities.
- Parents can track games and set time restrictions to maintain a healthy mix of online and offline activities.

3) Social Interaction

- Children may begin to use messaging applications to interact with friends and family under parental supervision. Messenger Kids and other apps provide a secure atmosphere for social engagement.
- These platforms include parental controls for monitoring and managing communication.

4) Watching Educational Videos

- Watching instructional films on platforms like YouTube and PBS Kids is still popular. These films cover a variety of topics and frequently feature interactive aspects.
- Parents should direct their children towards high-quality educational content.

C) Ages 10-12: Preteens

1) Conduct Online Research for School Projects

- Preteens utilize the internet to get information for school assignments and homework. They may access instructional websites, digital libraries, and online encyclopedias.
- Parents may teach their children to recognize reputable sources and check facts.

2) Social Media Introduction

- Preteens may develop an interest in social media sites such as Instagram, Snapchat, and TikTok. Parents should help their children create accounts and understand privacy settings.
- Discussions regarding appropriate social media use and associated consequences are critical at this point.

3) Online Gaming

- Multiplayer internet games like Fortnite and Among Us have gained popularity. These games encourage social interaction and

collaboration.
- Parents should watch their children's gaming activities and ensure that they behave appropriately online.

4) Content Creation

- Preteens may begin developing their content, such as videos or blogs, and express themselves creatively through platforms such as YouTube and TikTok.
- Parents should advise them on safe content creation techniques and the value of privacy.

D) Ages 13-16: Teenagers

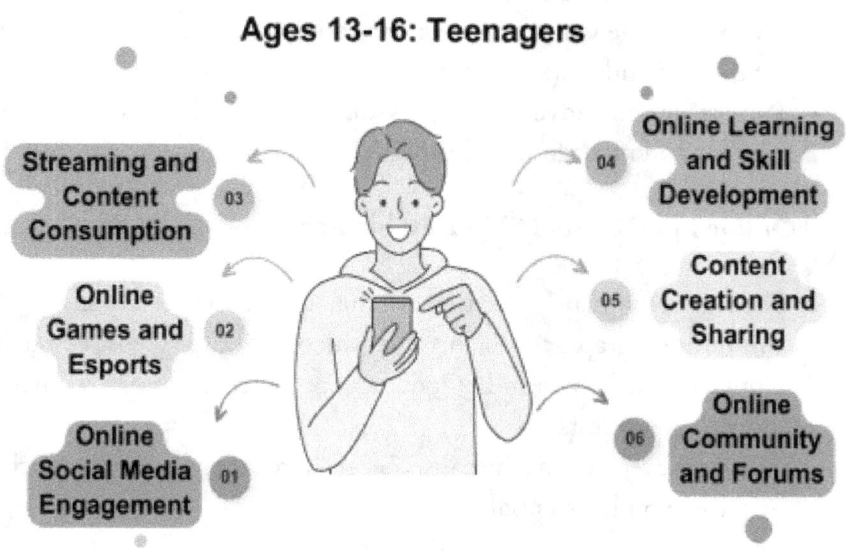

1) Social Media Engagement

- Teenagers are very active on social media sites such as Instagram, Snapchat, TikTok, and Twitter. They utilize these platforms to interact with their peers, discuss their experiences, and stay informed on trends.

- Parents should talk about digital footprints, online reputation, and the value of friendly relationships.

2) Online Games and Esports

- Online gaming remains a popular activity. League of Legends, Fortnite, and Call of Duty are popular among teenagers, and esports and competitive gaming communities capture their curiosity.
- Establishing limits and maintaining a good balance with other pursuits is critical.

3) Streaming and Content Consumption

- Teens commonly utilize streaming services such as Netflix, Hulu, and YouTube to view movies, television series, and videos. They also track influencers and content makers.
- Parents should advise teenagers on how to select age-appropriate content and manage screen time.

4) Online Learning and Skill Development

- Teenagers frequently use the Internet to acquire new skills, such as computing, graphic design, and video editing. Websites such as Coursera, Udemy, and Codecademy offer courses tailored to individual interests.
- Encourage teenagers to use internet resources productively, which can help them build essential skills for the future.

5) Content Creation and Sharing

- Many kids produce and distribute their material, including movies, music, and artwork. Platforms like YouTube, TikTok, and Instagram allow for creative expression.
- Parents should talk about the repercussions of sharing personal information online and promote responsible digital citizenship.

6) Online Community and Forums

- Teens frequently join online communities and forums based on their interests, such as Reddit, Discord, and specialized interest groups. These platforms promote social engagement and knowledge sharing.
- Parents should promote good participation while keeping an eye out for any negative encounters.

Understanding popular internet activities for different age groups allows parents to provide appropriate direction and assistance. By being aware and active, parents can help their children navigate the digital world securely and ethically, creating a balanced and rewarding online experience.

2.2 Trends in Kids Internet Usage

Understanding children's internet use patterns is critical for parents who want to keep ahead of the trends and provide their children with a secure and meaningful online experience. These trends focus on how youngsters interact with the digital environment and the changing landscape of online activities. Here are some significant trends in children's internet usage:

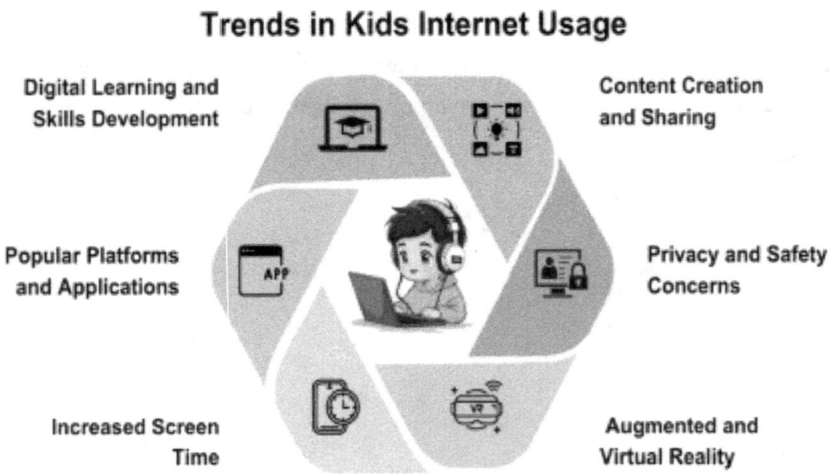

A) Increased Screen Time

1) Rising Screen Time for All Ages

- Over the last decade, children's screen usage has grown considerably. This increase is attributed to the spread of smartphones, tablets, and other technological devices.
- Children now spend an average of 3-5 hours a day watching screens, with older children and teens sometimes exceeding this figure.

2) Impact of Remote Learning

- The COVID-19 epidemic drove the trend toward more screen time as remote learning became necessary. Children spend more significant time online for educational objectives, such as taking virtual classes and using online resources.

- Even when schools return to in-person instruction, the use of digital technologies in education remains widespread.

B) Popular Platforms and Applications

1) Social Media Dominance

- TikTok, Instagram, and Snapchat are very popular among children and teens. These platforms combine entertainment, social engagement, and content development.
- TikTok, in particular, has experienced a significant spike in popularity, with its short-form video material appealing to a younger demographic.

2) Gaming and Interactive Entertainment

- Online gaming remains a popular trend, with platforms such as Roblox, Fortnite, and Minecraft leading the way. These games, which provide immersive experiences and social engagement, have attracted millions of young gamers.
- The emergence of esports and game streaming on sites such as Twitch has also helped to boost the popularity of online gaming.

3) Streaming Services

- Children frequently entertain themselves with streaming services like YouTube, Netflix, and Disney+. YouTube is popular due to its vast selection of material, which includes vlogs, tutorials, and game videos.
- Subscription streaming services provide age-appropriate content that parents may select.

C) Digital Learning and Skills Development

1) E-Learning Platforms

- The use of e-learning systems such as Khan Academy, Coursera, and Duolingo have grown. These platforms include courses and materials for a variety of ages and disciplines.
- Children use these sites to complement their school instruction and discover new hobbies.

2) Coding and STEM Education

- Children are becoming increasingly interested in coding and STEM education. Platforms such as Scratch, Code.org, and Tynker offer dynamic and exciting methods to learn programming and other STEM concepts.
- This trend illustrates the growing significance of digital literacy in the modern world.

D) Content Creation and Sharing

1) Rise of User-Generated Content

- Children and teens are becoming more interested in generating and sharing their material. YouTube, TikTok, and Instagram enable them to express their creativity through videos, music, and art.
- This trend demonstrates the move from passive consumption to active content generation.

2) Influencer Culture

- Online celebrities and influencers have a significant impact on younger audiences. Many young people admire and desire to be influencers themselves, generating material that connects with their peers.
- Parents should help their children understand the responsibilities and risks of becoming an online influencer.

E) Privacy and Safety Concerns

1) Growing Awareness of Privacy

- As kids become more engaged online, there is an increased awareness of privacy concerns. Many platforms have included tools to safeguard young users' privacy, such as limited profiles and content filtering.
- Parents should teach their children the value of privacy and how to handle their internet presence properly.

2) Cyberbullying and Online Harassment

- Despite growing awareness, cyberbullying and internet abuse remain serious issues. Children may face unfavorable interactions on social media and gaming sites.
- Parents should monitor their children's online interactions and offer advice on how to deal with cyberbullying.

F) Integration of Augmented and Virtual Reality

1) Emerging Technologies

- The integration of augmented reality (AR) and virtual reality (VR) into games and educational aids is gaining popularity. These technologies provide immersive experiences that can boost both learning and enjoyment.
- Platforms such as Oculus and AR-based instructional apps are growing increasingly popular among younger audiences.

2) Potential Benefits and Risks

- While AR and VR provide great options for learning and creativity, they also carry hazards such as motion sickness and prolonged screen time.
- Parents should make sure that these devices are utilized responsibly and in moderation.

Understanding patterns in children's internet usage allows parents to remain aware and proactive in directing their children's online experiences. Recognizing these tendencies allows parents to help their children better as they navigate the internet world securely and ethically. Staying active and informed about these changing trends is critical for creating a good and secure digital environment for children.

2.3 Statistical Overview of Kids Internet Usage

Understanding statistical trends in children's internet usage could offer helpful information for parents. This data shows how children and teens interact with digital devices and online platforms, which may help parents better supervise their children's digital activities. Here's a thorough statistical summary based on current research:

A) Digital Device Access and Usage

1) Smartphone Access

- **Teenagers (13-17):** A stunning 95% of teenagers own cell phones. This high rate of adoption demonstrates the critical role cell phones play in their daily lives.
- **Younger Children (8 years old):** The number of eight-year-olds having phones has risen from 11% in 2015 to 31% in 2023, demonstrating that mobile technology is becoming more accessible to younger children.

2) Computers and Tablets

- **Desktops/Laptops:** 90% of teenagers have access to desktop or laptop computers, which are essential for schooling.
- **Tablets:** 65% of teenagers have access to tablets, which are helpful for both study and enjoyment.

3) Gaming consoles

- **General Access:** 83% of teenagers use gaming consoles, demonstrating the popularity of gaming as an entertainment pastime.
- **Gender Disparity:** Boys (91%) have more access to gaming consoles than females (75%).

4) Income Differences in Device Access

- **Lower-Income Households:** In low-income households, 72% of teenagers have access to computers.
- **Middle-Income Households:** 87% of middle-income households have access to a computer.
- **Higher-Income Households:** 94% of higher-income households have access to a computer.

In contrast to PC access, smartphone access is relatively evenly distributed across socioeconomic levels.

B) Internet Usage Patterns

1) Frequency of Internet Use

- **Daily Use:** 96% of teens say they use the internet every day.
- **Constant Use:** 46% of teens spend nearly all of their time online, up from 24% in 2015.

2) Variations by Age and Demographics

- **Older teens (15-17):** 50% say they are virtually always online.
- **Younger teenagers:** 40% claim continual internet use.
- **Racial/Ethnic Differences:** White kids (38%) are less likely to report being always online than Black teens (54%) or Latinx teens (55%).

3) Impact on Daily Life

- **Disregard of Responsibilities:** According to recent research, 61% of teens use technology, which causes them to disregard everyday tasks on occasion or frequently.
- **Sleep Disruption:** 67% of teens report lacking sleep as a result of late-night internet use.

C) Smartphone Usage Details

1) Daily Usage Time

- **Average Use:** Teenagers (aged 11 to 17) spend more than 4.5 hours each day on cell phones.
- **Frequency of Use:** The average daily smartphone pickup is 51 times, with 44% of older teens (16-17) picking up their phones more than 100 times.

2) Notifications

- **Daily Notifications:** Over half of teens receive more than 200 notifications every day.
- **School Hours:** 23% of notifications are delivered during school hours, and 5% during school night hours.

3) Primary Activities

- **Social Media:** Social media applications account for 42% of smartphone use.
- **YouTube:** Video viewing accounts for 19% of all usage.
- **Mobile Games:** Mobile gaming accounts for 11% of total use.

D) Social Interaction and Development

1) Texting

- **Usage:** High school kids routinely text their classmates, peers, and love partners, and they communicate with their parents on occasion.

2) Social Media Platforms

- **Popular Platforms:** Popular platforms include YouTube (93%), TikTok (63%), Snapchat (60%), Instagram (59%), Facebook (33%), and Discord (28%).
- **Daily Visits:** YouTube (71%), TikTok (58%), Snapchat (51%), and Instagram (47%) are visited daily.

3) Digital Media and Bullying

- **Cyberbullying Incidence:** 23% of teenagers were bullied online in the previous month, up from 16% in 2016.
- **Demographic Variations:** Transgender (35%) and LGBTQ (32%) youth had higher rates than non-LGBTQ youth (22%).

E) Entertainment and Health Information

1) Video Watching

- **Daily Viewership:** 77% of teenagers watch videos online every day.
- **Popular Platforms:** The top options are Netflix and YouTube.

2) Gaming

- **Gender Differences:** 60% of males and 24% of girls aged 8 to 18 say they love playing video games "a lot."
- **Average Time:** Teen guys spend about 2.5 hours each day gaming, while teen girls spend only one hour.

3) Pornography Exposure

- **Exposure rates:** 73% of teenagers have seen pornography by the age of 17, and 54% by the age of 13.
- **Intentional Viewing:** Intentional viewing is higher among cisgender boys (52%) and transgender/nonbinary kids (66%) than cisgender girls (36%).

4) Health Information

- **Online Health Resources:** 87% of teenagers and young adults use the internet for health information, with an emphasis on exercise, diet, stress, anxiety, and depression.
- **Health Applications:** Nearly half (49%) of teenagers use mobile health applications.

These statistics highlight the prevalence of digital technology and the Internet in the lives of children and teenagers. Understanding these use patterns and trends allows parents to make more educated decisions regarding their children's internet activity. By being aware and active, parents can guarantee that their children benefit from the positive features of the digital world while minimizing potential risks associated with excessive or dangerous internet use.

2.4 The Role of Social Media in Kid's Lives

Social media has become an integral part of children's and teens' lives, significantly impacting how they interact, study, and enjoy themselves. Understanding the significance of social media in children's lives is critical for parents in guiding their children toward healthy and secure online interactions. Here are some essential features of how social media affects young users:

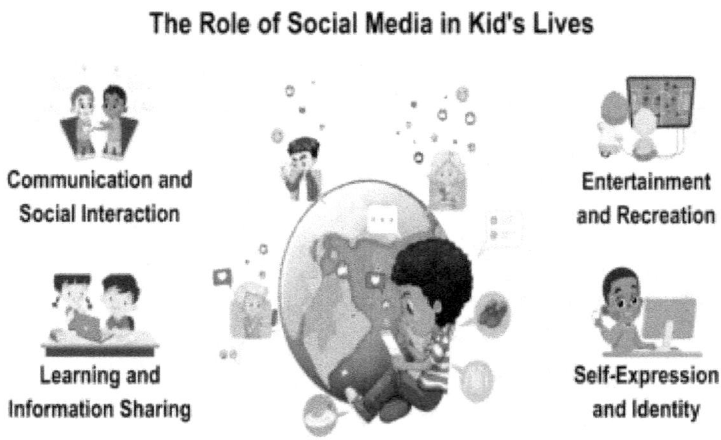

A) Communication and Social Interaction

1) Staying in Touch with Friends and Family

- Social media services such as Instagram, Snapchat, and TikTok allow children and teens to keep in touch with their friends and family members. These technologies allow for real-time connections through texting, videoconferencing, and sharing updates.
- Many children, particularly teens, use social media as their primary way of maintaining relationships and socializing.

2) Creating New Friendships

- Social media enables children to meet and interact with new individuals who share their interests. Online networks and clubs can help children make friends outside their local surroundings.
- Platforms such as Discord and Reddit allow young people to discuss their hobbies and interests, establishing a sense of belonging and community.

3) Peer Support and Empathy

- Social media can serve as a form of peer support, allowing youngsters to share their experiences and advice. This might be especially helpful for individuals who feel lonely or suffer difficulties in their offline lives.
- Positive connections on social media can promote empathy and understanding among peers.

B) Learning and Information Sharing

1) Access to Educational Content

- Many social media networks include instructional information that children may access. YouTube channels, for example, provide lessons in science, math, art, and music.
- Influencers and educators on platforms such as Instagram and TikTok generate educational material, making learning more entertaining and accessible.

2) Awareness of Current Events

- Teenagers rely heavily on social media to stay informed about current events. They utilize sites like Twitter and Facebook to stay up to date on global and local news.
- Understanding how to analyze the content they come across on social media critically is vital for creating educated and accountable digital citizens.

3) Sharing Knowledge and Creativity

- Children use social media to share their knowledge and creativity with a larger audience. Platforms such as YouTube and TikTok enable children to produce and upload videos exhibiting their abilities, interests, and instructional information.
- Sharing information might build their confidence and motivate them to pursue their hobbies further.

C) Entertainment and Recreation

1) Consumption of Entertaining Content

- TikTok, YouTube, and Instagram are popular sources of entertainment for youngsters. They watch videos, follow their favorite influencers, and take part in trendy challenges.
- Consumption of material gives relaxation and enjoyment, but screen time must be balanced with other activities.

2) Participating in Online Challenges and Trends

- Social media trends and difficulties frequently attract the curiosity of kids and teens. Participating in these activities can be enjoyable and exciting, but they can also offer potential risks if the challenges are unsafe or improper.
- Parents should monitor their children's participation in various challenges and address potential risk factors.

D) Self-Expression and Identity

1) Exploring and Expressing Identity

- Social media allows kids to discover and express their identities. They may spread their ideas, experiences, and creative works to a larger audience.
- This discovery is a natural part of growing up, but parents must help their children protect their privacy and make safe decisions about what they share online.

2) Influence on Self-Esteem and Body Image

- The information that kids see on social media may have a substantial influence on their self-esteem and body image. Comparisons to idealized pictures and lifestyles might evoke emotions of inadequacy or pressure to comply.
- Parents should encourage frank discussions about self-worth and the false nature of many internet depictions to help their children develop a positive self-image.

Social media has a complex impact on the lives of children and teens. It provides possibilities for communication, learning, and self-expression but also poses substantial obstacles and threats. Understanding these dynamics allows parents to better guide their children through pleasant and safe social media interactions. Open communication, monitoring, and instruction about safe online conduct are essential tactics for guiding children through the complicated world of social media.

2.5 Online Gaming: Benefits and Risks

Online gaming has grown popular among children and teens, providing a combination of enjoyment, social connection, and cognitive growth. However, it does carry some concerns that parents should be aware of. Understanding the positive and negative aspects of online gaming can assist parents in guiding their children through a balanced and safe gaming experience. Here are the main features of internet gaming for kids:

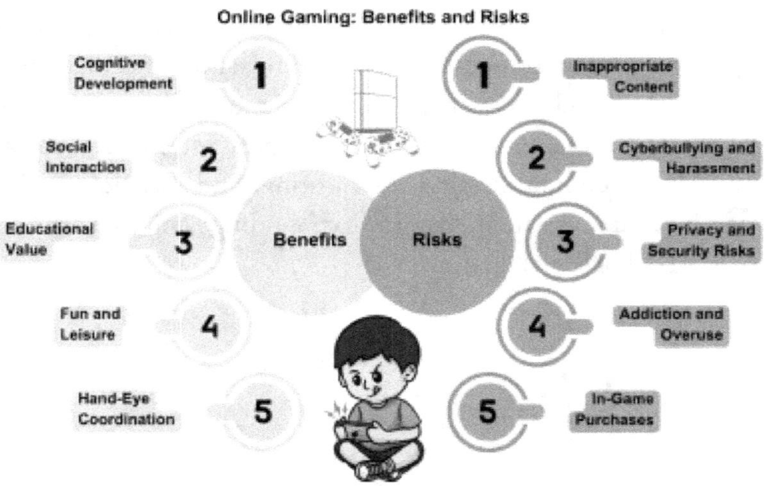

A) Benefits of Online Gaming

1) Cognitive Development

- **Problem-Solving Skills:** Many online games demand players to solve puzzles, complete tasks, and overcome obstacles, which helps them improve their problem-solving and critical thinking skills.
- **Strategic Thinking:** Chess, strategy games, and role-playing games (RPGs) all motivate players to plan, strategize, and think ahead, which helps to develop strategic thinking and planning abilities.

2) Social Interaction

- **Building Friendships:** Online multiplayer games allow youngsters to interact with their classmates and establish new friends. These games frequently call for collaboration and cooperation, which can aid in the development of social skills.
- **Global Connectivity:** Players from all around the world may engage and cooperate, gaining exposure to a variety of cultures and viewpoints.

3) Educational Value

- **Learning through Play:** Educational games can make learning enjoyable and interesting. Games that focus on math, science, and history help students learn more in the classroom.
- **Skill Development:** Many games use interactive gameplay to teach practical skills like typing, coding, and even learning a new language.

4) Fun and leisure

- **Stress Relief:** Gaming can help kids relax and release tension after a hard day at school.
- **Creativity and Imagination:** Sandbox games such as Minecraft allow kids to build and design their worlds, which promotes creativity and imagination.

5) Hand-Eye Coordination

- **Reflexes and Coordination**: Fast-paced games increase hand-eye coordination and reflexes, which can be helpful in physical activity and other situations.

B) Risks of Online Gaming

1) Exposure to Inappropriate Content

- **Violence and Explicit Content:** Certain games include violent or explicit content that may be inappropriate for minors. Parents should examine the game ratings and content.

- **Immoderate Interactions:** Children in online gaming situations may be exposed to improper language and conduct from other gamers.

2) Cyberbullying and Harassment

- **Online Harassment:** Children may experience bullying, harassment, or toxic conduct from other gamers. This may have a detrimental influence on their mental health and self-esteem.
- **Reporting and Blocking:** Parents should teach their children how to report and block abusive gamers while also encouraging open discussion about their online experiences.

3) Privacy and Security Risks

- **Personal Information:** Some games demand personal information to create an account. Children may unknowingly reveal critical information to strangers.
- **Phishing and Scams:** Scammers might target kids with phishing attacks and fraudulent schemes. Educating kids about online safety is critical.

4) Addiction and Overuse

- **Excessive Screen Time:** Gaming for too long can lead to screen addiction, which can have a negative influence on physical health, sleep quality, and academic achievement.
- **Balance and Moderation:** Setting time restrictions and encouraging breaks might help you strike a good balance between gaming and other tasks.

5) In-Game Purchases

- **Micro-Transactions:** Many games have in-game purchases, which might result in unintentional expenditure. Children may only partially appreciate the real-world expense of these purchases.

- **Parental Controls:** It is critical to use parental controls to regulate in-game spending and to teach kids the value of responsible spending.

Online gaming has several advantages, including cognitive growth, social connection, and educational value. However, it also carries concerns like exposure to unsuitable information, cyberbullying, and addiction. By recognizing both benefits and risks, parents may help their children have a happy and balanced gaming experience. Active engagement, setting boundaries, promoting a range of activities, and teaching about online safety are all essential tactics for guiding kids through the world of online gaming securely and ethically.

2.6 Streaming and Content Consumption

In the digital age, streaming services and internet material have become an essential aspect of children's lives. Understanding the principles of streaming and content consumption can assist parents in guiding their children to safe and good watching habits. Here are some significant features of how streaming and content consumption affect children:

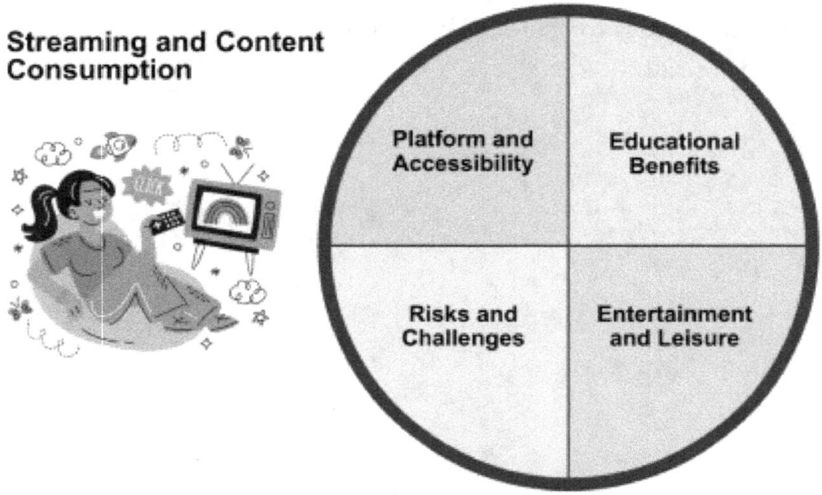

A) Platform and Accessibility

1) Popular Streaming Platforms

- **YouTube:** YouTube is a popular website where children may watch a wide range of information, including instructional videos, entertainment, and lessons.
- **Netflix and Disney+:** Netflix and Disney+ are subscription-based services that provide a vast collection of movies, television series, and unique material appropriate for various age groups.
- **Hulu and Amazon Prime Video:** Hulu and Amazon Prime Video are other popular services that provide a variety of entertainment alternatives for children and families.

2) Easy Access

- **Smart Devices:** Children may access streaming services using smartphones, tablets, smart TVs, and gaming consoles, making material accessible at any time.
- **Internet Connectivity:** As high-speed internet became more widespread, streaming quality and accessibility increased, promoting more regular use.

B) Educational Benefits

1) Learning Resources

- **Educational Channels:** Platforms such as YouTube have channels dedicated to educational programming, which covers topics such as science, history, and arithmetic. Channels such as Khan Academy and National Geographic Kids offer excellent learning opportunities.
- **Documentaries and Shows:** Streaming services include documentaries and educational shows that can help kids learn a variety of topics and promote a passion for learning.

2) Interactive Content

- **Edutainment:** Interactive shows and applications blend education and entertainment, making learning more exciting and enjoyable. Programs like Sesame Street and Blue's Clues are examples of educational content that is also entertaining.
- **Language Learning:** Streaming services provide content in different languages, enabling youngsters to learn new languages and enhance their language abilities.

C) Entertainment and Leisure

1) Entertainment Options

- **Movies and TV Series:** Streaming services provide a diverse selection of movies and television series to appeal to people of all ages and interests. Animated movies, superhero pictures, and adventure series are top-rated among children.

- **Music and Dance:** Platforms such as YouTube and TikTok provide music videos and dance instructions, allowing kids to enjoy and engage in these activities.

2) Stress Reduction and Relaxation

- **Comfort Viewing:** After a long day, kids can relax by watching their favorite shows and movies. It offers some time off from schooling and additional obligations.
- **Mindfulness Information:** Some platforms include information about mindfulness and relaxation to assist kids in handling stress and anxiety.

D) Risks and Challenges

1) Exposure to Unsuitable Material

- **Unfiltered Content:** Despite content filters, children may encounter unsuitable or unsafe information. This includes any violent, sexual, or distressing content that is inappropriate for their age.
- **User-Generated Material:** Platforms such as YouTube host user-generated material, which can vary significantly in quality and relevance. Some material makers may need to follow appropriate rules for kids.

2) Overconsumption and Screen Time

- **Excessive Viewing:** Using streaming services for an extended period can lead to screen addiction, which can have an impact on physical health, sleep habits, and academic performance.
- **Physical Inactivity:** Extended durations of sedentary watching can lead to a lack of physical activity, which can affect overall health and fitness.

3) Advertisements and influences

- **Targeted Ads:** Children may be exposed to targeted marketing, which influences their purchasing decisions and preferences. These advertisements may promote unhealthy foods, toys, or other goods.
- **Influencer Content:** Influencers on platforms such as YouTube can influence children's perceptions and behavior. It is critical to monitor the influences children follow and the messages they take in.

Streaming and content consumption provide various benefits, including educational value, amusement, and relaxation. However, they also raise concerns about improper material, overconsumption, and the effect of targeted ads. By recognizing these dynamics and employing appropriate parenting measures, parents may help their children have a balanced and fulfilling streaming experience. Setting boundaries, promoting a range of activities, co-viewing content, and keeping open communication are essential for creating a secure and happy digital environment for children.

Chapter 3: Devices Used by Kids to Access the Internet

In the digital age, children and teenagers are growing up surrounded by a number of devices that connect them to the internet, each playing an essential role in their daily lives. These devices—ranging from smartphones and tablets to laptops, desktops, gaming consoles, smart TVs, and even wearable technology—have become essential tools for education, communication, entertainment, and social interaction. The widespread availability and accessibility of these technologies have profoundly transformed the way young people engage with the world around them, offering outstanding opportunities for learning and growth. While they also introduce a new set of challenges and risks that parents must understand, it is essential to remember the positive impact these devices can have on a child's development.

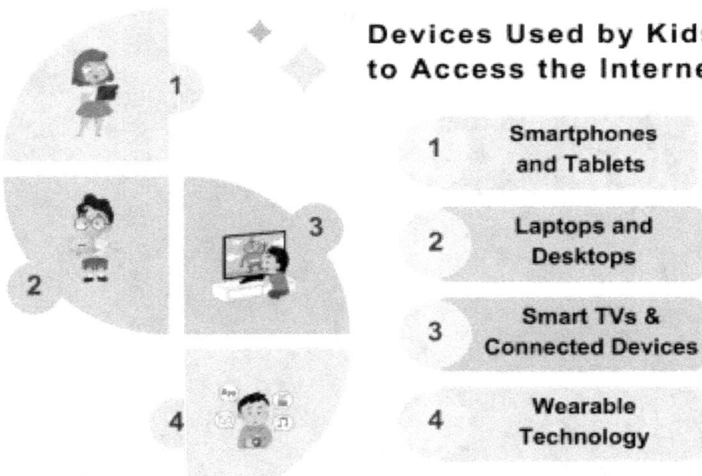

Smartphones and Tablets

Smartphones, often a child's first personal device, provide constant connectivity and access to social media, games, and a vast range of apps. While these devices offer incredible convenience and a gateway to information, they also raise concerns about privacy, exposure to inappropriate content, and the risk of cyberbullying. Tablets, with their larger screens and interactive capabilities, serve as versatile tools for both learning and relaxation. Still, they can also lead to overreliance on digital content and reduced physical activity.

Laptops and Desktops

Laptops and desktops, traditionally seen as essential for academic purposes, are now multifunctional hubs that support everything from homework and research to gaming and streaming. These devices are integral to developing digital literacy skills, yet they also pose risks such as exposure to harmful content, cyber threats, and the challenge of managing screen time. Gaming consoles, which are immensely popular among children and teenagers, offer a unique blend of entertainment and social interaction. However, the captivating nature of these games, connected with the potential for exposure to violent content and in-game purchases, requires careful oversight.

Smart TVs and Other Connectable Devices

Smart TVs and other connected devices, like streaming sticks and smart speakers, have further expanded the digital ecosystem in the home. These devices provide easy access to a wide range of content but also raise significant concerns about privacy, data security, and the potential for excessive screen time.

Wearable Technology

Finally, the emergence of wearable technology and the Internet of Things (IoT) has added another layer of complexity to the digital landscape. Devices like smartwatches and internet-connected toys are designed to integrate seamlessly into daily life, offering both convenience and educational benefits but also introducing new privacy and security challenges.

As these devices become increasingly connected with the lives of children, the responsibility of managing their use falls heavily on parents. This is not a burden but an opportunity for parents to guide their children's digital experiences. The challenges associated with these technologies are various, affecting not only the safety and privacy of children but also their physical and mental well-being. This chapter aims to provide a comprehensive overview of the various devices that children use to access the internet, examining the benefits they offer while also highlighting the potential risks they pose. With the proper guidance, parents can ensure that their children's digital experiences are safe, educational, and enjoyable.

By understanding the role of each device in a child's life, parents can gain valuable insights into how these technologies influence their children's behavior, development, and overall digital experience. As we explore each device in detail, we will discuss how they are used, the potential issues associated with their use, and the ways in which they shape the digital landscape that today's children must learn. This chapter serves as a foundation for the subsequent discussion in the next chapter, where we will discuss in detail the specific challenges and risks these devices introduce and explore their broader impact on children's digital lives. We understand that navigating this digital landscape can be complex, but with the proper knowledge and support, parents can ensure that their children have a positive digital experience.

3.1 Smartphones

Smartphones have become an integral part of modern life, and this is particularly true for children and teenagers. As one of the most accessible and widely used devices, smartphones offer a world of possibilities, from communication and entertainment to education and social interaction. However, their widespread presence in the lives of young people also brings a range of issues, challenges, and risks that parents need to be aware of.

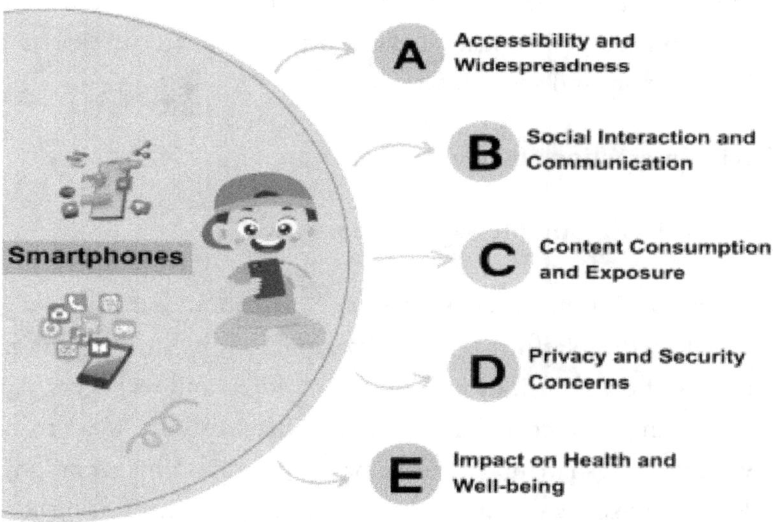

A) Accessibility and Widespreadness

1. Widespread Ownership

- **Prevalence among Children:** A significant number of children and teenagers own or have access to smartphones. Research indicates that nearly 95% of teens between the ages of 13 and 17 have a smartphone, making it the most common device used by this age group.
- **Younger Age of Ownership:** The age at which children first get their smartphone is decreasing. Many children now receive their first smartphone by the age of 10 or even younger, which has profound

implications for their digital lives.

1. **Constant Connectivity**

- **Always Online:** Smartphones provide children with constant access to the internet, social media, games, and apps. This connectivity means they are always online, often checking their devices throughout the day and even during the night.
- **Dependency on Smartphones:** Many children develop a strong attachment to their smartphones, using them not only for communication but also as their primary source of entertainment, information, and social interaction.

B) Social Interaction and Communication

1. **Social Media and Messaging Apps**

- **Primary Communication Tools:** Smartphones are the gateway to social media platforms and messaging apps, which are the primary means of communication for many children and teenagers. Apps like Instagram, Snapchat, TikTok, and WhatsApp are used to connect with friends, share updates, and participate in online communities.
- **Pressure to Stay Connected:** The social dynamics of being constantly connected can create pressure for children to remain active on these platforms, often leading to concerns about social status, peer approval, and fear of missing out (FOMO).

1. **Cyberbullying and Online Harassment**

- **Increased Risk:** The widespread use of smartphones for communication also increases the risk of cyberbullying and online harassment. Children may experience or witness bullying through social media, messaging apps, or group chats, which can have severe emotional and psychological effects.
- **Lack of Escape:** Unlike traditional forms of bullying, cyberbullying follows children into their homes through their smartphones, making

it difficult to escape the negative effects and contributing to increased anxiety and stress.

C) Content Consumption and Exposure

1. **Access to Inappropriate Content**

- **Unfiltered Access:** With a smartphone, children have easy access to a vast amount of online content, some of which may be inappropriate for their age. This includes exposure to violent, explicit, or harmful material that can negatively impact their development and worldview.
- **Difficulties in Monitoring:** Smartphones' portability and personal nature make it challenging for parents to monitor what their children are viewing, particularly when content is consumed in private.

1. **Influence of Social Media**

- **Impact on Self-Esteem:** Social media platforms accessible through smartphones can significantly influence children's self-esteem and body image. Constantly comparing idealized images and lifestyles on these platforms can lead to feelings of inadequacy and dissatisfaction.
- **Spread of Misinformation:** Smartphones also expose children to misinformation and harmful content shared on social media. With proper guidance, children may be able to discern credible information from falsehoods, leading to misconceptions and confusion.

D) Privacy and Security Concerns

1. **Data Privacy Risks**

- **Personal Data Collection:** Smartphones are equipped with apps that collect vast amounts of personal data, including location, browsing history, and usage patterns. Children, often unaware of these practices, may unknowingly share sensitive information that could be exploited.
- **Inadequate Understanding of Privacy Settings:** Many children need help understanding or utilizing the privacy settings available on

their smartphones, which can leave them vulnerable to data breaches, identity theft, or unauthorized access to their personal information.

1. **Online Predators**

- **Vulnerability to Exploitation:** Smartphones' anonymity can make children vulnerable to online predators who may use social media, messaging apps, or games to initiate contact and exploit them. This is a significant risk, particularly for younger children who may not recognize the dangers of interacting with strangers online.
- **Challenges in Detection:** The private nature of smartphone use can make it difficult for parents to detect when an online predator is targeting their child, further complicating the task of keeping them safe.

E) Impact on Health and Well-being

1. **Screen Time and Addiction**

- **Excessive Use:** Smartphone's convenience and appeal can lead to excessive screen time, with children spending hours each day on their devices. This overuse can contribute to various health issues, including eye strain, poor posture, and disrupted sleep patterns.
- **Addictive Behaviors:** The design of many apps and games, which include elements of instant gratification and continuous engagement, can lead to addictive behaviors in children, making it difficult for them to disconnect from their devices.

1. **Mental Health Concerns**

- **Increased Anxiety and Depression:** The pressures associated with social media use, cyberbullying, and constant connectivity can contribute to increased levels of anxiety and depression in children. The need to present a perfect image online, associated with negative interactions, can take a toll on their mental health.
- **Disrupted Sleep Patterns:** Many children use their smartphones late

into the night, leading to sleep lack and fatigue. The blue light emitted by screens can also interfere with their sleep cycles, further heightening these issues.

Smartphones have become a central device in the lives of children, providing them with remarkable access to information, communication, and entertainment. However, this accessibility comes with significant challenges and risks that parents must be aware of. From exposure to inappropriate content and cyberbullying to privacy concerns and health impacts, the use of smartphones by children presents a complex set of issues that require careful consideration. Understanding these challenges is the first step in helping parents navigate the digital world alongside their children, ensuring their safety and well-being in the process.

3.2 Tablets

Tablets have become increasingly popular among children for their versatility, portability, and user-friendly interfaces. These devices serve as a bridge between smartphones and computers, offering a wide range of functionalities that serve both educational and recreational needs. However, like all digital devices, tablets come with their own set of challenges and risks that parents need to be aware of.

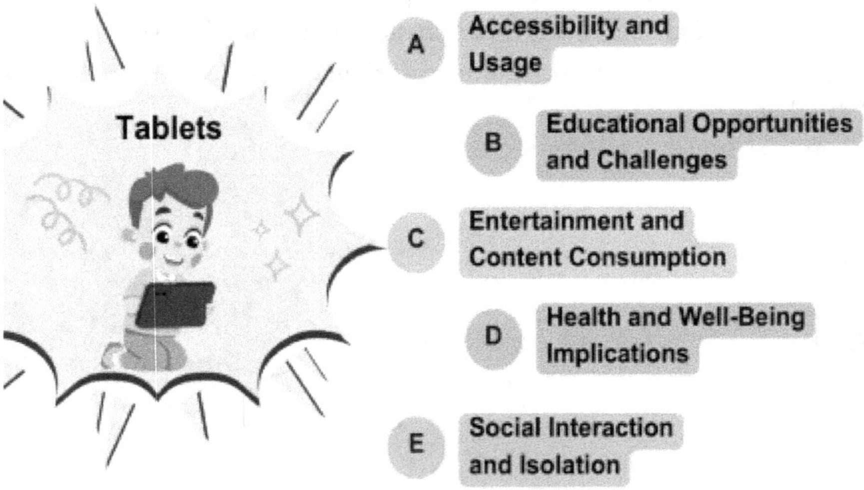

A) Accessibility and Usage

1. **Widespread Adoption**

- **Majority among Younger Children:** Tablets are top-rated among younger children, often serving as their first introduction to digital devices. The touch interfaces and the availability of child-friendly apps make tablets an appealing choice for both kids and parents.
- **Multi-Use Device:** Tablets are often used for a variety of purposes, including watching videos, playing games, reading e-books, and accessing educational content. This multi-functionality makes them a central device in many households.

1. **Ease of Use**

- **User-Friendly Design:** Tablets are designed to be easy to use, with large screens and simple navigation that are ideal for children. This ease of use encourages frequent interaction with the device, often leading to extended periods of screen time.
- **Portability:** Tablets are portable, so children can use them anywhere, whether at home, in the car, or even at school. This constant availability increases the likelihood of frequent and extended use.

B) Educational Opportunities and Challenges

1. **Access to Educational Content**

- **Learning Apps and E-Books:** Tablets are often loaded with educational apps and e-books that cater to various age groups and learning levels. These resources can support school learning, enhance literacy, and encourage curiosity in subjects like math, science, and reading.
- **Interactive Learning:** Many educational apps on tablets offer interactive experiences that engage children in active learning. These apps often include quizzes, games, and challenges that make learning fun and engaging.

1. **Over-Reliance on Digital Learning**

- **Screen-Based Learning:** While tablets offer valuable educational tools, there is a risk that children may become overly reliant on screen-based learning at the expense of other important developmental activities. Physical play, hands-on learning, and face-to-face social interactions are crucial for a well-rounded education.
- **Quality of Content:** Not all educational apps and content available on tablets are of high quality. Parents may need help to differentiate between genuinely educational content and apps that are merely entertaining without offering significant learning value.

C) Entertainment and Content Consumption

1. **Video Streaming and Games**

- **Access to Streaming Services:** Tablets are commonly used to access streaming services like YouTube, Netflix, and Disney+. These platforms offer a wide range of content, from educational videos to movies and TV shows. However, the vast amount of available content also includes material that may not be age-appropriate.
- **Gaming on Tablets:** Many children use tablets to play games, ranging from simple puzzles to more complex interactive experiences. While gaming can be educational and entertaining, it can also lead to excessive screen time and potential exposure to inappropriate content.

1. **Content Filtering Challenges**

- **Difficulty Monitoring Content:** Tablets, with their portability and personal use, make it difficult for parents to monitor the content their children consume. Children may easily access videos, games, or apps that are not suitable for their age, especially if appropriate content filters need to be put in place.
- **Advertisements and In-App Purchases:** Many free apps and games on tablets are supported by advertisements or include in-app purchases. These can expose children to targeted ads or lead to unintentional purchases, creating both financial and ethical concerns.

D) Health and Well-Being Implications

1. **Physical Health Concerns**

- **Eye Strain and Posture Issues:** Prolonged tablet use can lead to eye strain, especially if children hold the device close to their face or use it in low-light conditions. Poor posture while using tablets, such as reclining or lying down, can also contribute to physical discomfort or long-term posture issues.
- **Reduced Physical Activity:** Tablet's engaging nature can result in

children spending significant amounts of time sitting still, reducing their opportunities for physical exercise. This inactive behavior can have implications for their overall health and development.

1. **Sleep Disruption**

- **Blue Light Exposure:** Tablet screens emit blue light, which can interfere with the production of melatonin, the hormone responsible for regulating sleep. Using tablets, especially in the hours before bedtime, can disrupt children's sleep patterns, leading to difficulties falling asleep and reduced sleep quality.
- **Sleep Dependency:** Some children develop a habit of using tablets to fall asleep, relying on videos or games as part of their bedtime routine. This dependency can make it difficult for them to fall asleep without the device and can lead to further sleep disruptions.

E) Social Interaction and Isolation

1. **Solo Device Usage**

- **Individualized Experience:** Unlike other forms of technology that may encourage social interaction, such as multiplayer video games or family television watching, tablets are often used alone. This individual use can lead to isolation, as children may spend more time with their devices than interacting with family and friends.
- **Decreased Face-to-Face Interaction:** Over-reliance on tablets for entertainment and learning can reduce the time children spend engaging in face-to-face interactions. This can impact their social development, as real-world communication skills are crucial for building relationships and emotional intelligence.

1. **Impact on Family Dynamics**

- **Disruption of Family Time:** The ease of access to tablets can disrupt family routines, such as meal times or family outings. Children may prefer to use their tablets rather than participate in family activities, leading to a sense of disconnection within the household.

- **Parental Oversight Challenges:** Tablets can make it more difficult for parents to oversee all aspects of their children's digital lives, mainly when multiple devices are being used in different parts of the home. This lack of oversight can lead to concerns about the content being consumed and the habits being formed.

Tablets offer a versatile platform for both learning and entertainment, making them a popular choice for children of all ages. However, the widespread use of tablets also introduces several challenges and risks, from exposure to inappropriate content and physical health concerns to issues of social isolation and disrupted family dynamics. Understanding these challenges is essential for parents who wish to understand the complexities of tablet use in their children's lives. By being aware of the potential risks associated with tablet use, parents can better prepare themselves to guide their children in making safe and healthy choices in the digital world.

3.3 Laptops and Desktops

Laptops and desktops are fundamental tools in today's digital landscape, especially for children and teenagers. These devices are essential for educational purposes, creative projects, gaming, and social interaction. However, the widespread use of laptops and desktops also presents several challenges and risks that parents need to be aware of, particularly when it comes to managing their children's digital activities.

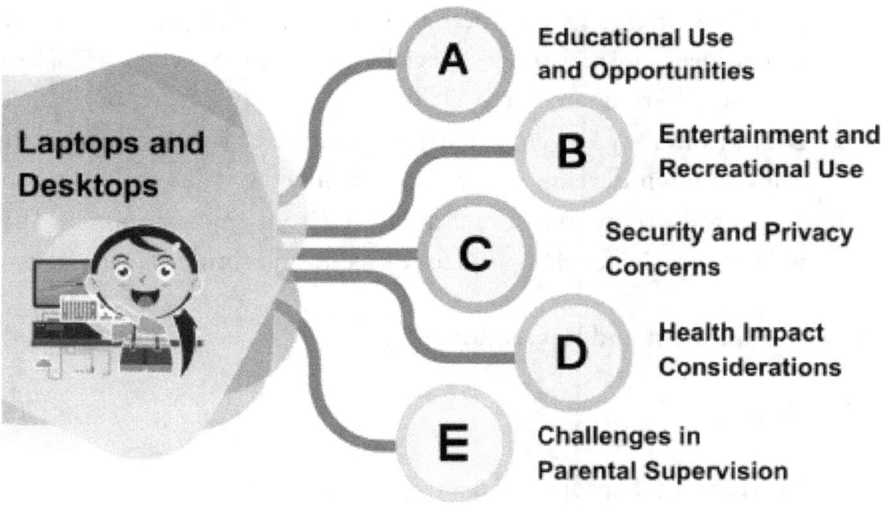

A) Educational Use and Opportunities

1. **Academic Tools**

- **Homework and Research:** Children often use laptops and desktops for school-related tasks such as writing essays, conducting research, and completing assignments. These devices provide access to a wealth of information and resources that can enhance learning and academic performance.
- **Educational Software and Applications:** Many educational programs and applications are specifically designed for laptops and

desktops. They offer interactive learning experiences in subjects like mathematics, science, and languages. These tools can supplement classroom learning and provide additional support for students who need it.

1. **E-Learning and Virtual Classrooms**

- **Access to Online Courses:** With the rise of e-learning platforms, laptops and desktops are increasingly being used to access online courses and virtual classrooms. These devices allow children to participate in lessons, complete assignments, and engage with teachers and students in real time, especially in situations where traditional classroom settings are not available.
- **Digital Literacy Development:** Regular use of laptops and desktops helps children develop essential digital literacy skills, such as typing, using productivity software, and learning from online resources. These skills are crucial for their academic success and future careers.

B) Entertainment and Recreational Use

1. **Gaming**

- **PC Gaming:** Laptops and desktops are popular platforms for gaming, particularly for more complex and graphics-intensive games. PC gaming often involves multiplayer online games, where children can interact with friends and other players worldwide. While gaming can be a fun and engaging activity, it also presents risks related to excessive screen time, exposure to inappropriate content, and interaction with strangers.
- **Creative Gaming and Modding:** Some children use laptops and desktops to explore creative aspects of gaming, such as modding (modifying game content) or creating their games. While these activities can develop technical skills and creativity, they also require a level of technical understanding and caution to avoid potential security risks.

1. **Streaming and Media Consumption**

- **Access to Streaming Services:** Laptops and desktops provide easy access to streaming services such as Netflix, YouTube, and Twitch. Children can watch movies, TV shows, and videos, as well as live-streamed content from their favorite creators. While this offers a vast array of entertainment options, it also raises concerns about the content being consumed, mainly if it needs to be age-appropriate.
- **Music and Video Creation:** These devices are also used for creative efforts such as music production, video editing, and graphic design. These activities can be highly beneficial for developing creative skills, but they require appropriate software and guidance to ensure children are using these tools safely and effectively.

C) Security and Privacy Concerns

1. **Data Security Risks**

- **Vulnerability to Malware and Viruses:** Laptops and desktops are susceptible to malware, viruses, and other cybersecurity threats. Children, who may not be fully aware of safe browsing practices, are at risk of unintentionally downloading harmful software or falling victim to phishing scams. This can lead to data breaches, identity theft, or loss of essential files.
- **Unsecured Networks:** Children may connect their laptops or desktops to unsecured Wi-Fi networks, mainly when they are using these devices outside the home, such as in a public library or a friend's house. This increases the risk of unauthorized access to their device and personal information.

1. **Online Privacy**

- **Personal Information Exposure:** Many websites and online platforms require users to provide personal information to create accounts or access services. Children may need to fully understand the importance of protecting their data, leading to unnecessary sharing of sensitive information such as their full name, address, or school details.

- **Social Media and Privacy Settings:** Laptops and desktops are often used to access social media platforms where children might share personal updates, photos, and videos. If privacy settings are not correctly set, strangers can access this information, leading to potential privacy violations and online safety risks.

D) Health Impact Considerations

1. Physical Health Concerns

- **Eye Strain and Ergonomics:** Prolonged use of laptops and desktops can lead to eye strain, mainly if children spend long hours staring at the screen without breaks. Additionally, improper ergonomics—such as poor posture, using an inappropriate chair, or placing the screen at the wrong height—can contribute to physical discomfort and long-term muscular and posture issues.
- **Lack of Physical Activity:** Extended periods spent on laptops and desktops often mean reduced physical activity. This sedentary behavior can lead to health issues such as obesity, poor circulatory health, and weakened muscle strength.

1. Mental Health Impact

- **Stress and Anxiety:** The academic and social pressures associated with using laptops and desktops can contribute to stress and anxiety in children. This is especially true when they are overwhelmed by schoolwork, online interactions, or negative experiences such as cyberbullying.
- **Sleep Disruption:** Using laptops and desktops late into the night can disrupt children's sleep patterns, mainly because the blue light emitted by screens interferes with the production of melatonin. This can lead to difficulties falling asleep, reduced sleep quality, and overall fatigue.

E) Challenges in Parental Supervision

1. **Difficulty in Monitoring Usage**

- **Private Use of Devices:** Laptops and desktops are often used in private spaces, such as a child's bedroom or personal study area, making it difficult for parents to monitor what their children are doing online. This lack of visibility can lead to concerns about the types of content being accessed and the amount of time spent on the device.
- **Complexity of Content Filtering:** While parental controls and content filtering tools are available for laptops and desktops, these tools can be complex to set up and manage. Additionally, tech-savvy children may find ways to bypass these controls, further complicating efforts to ensure safe usage.

1. **Balancing Freedom and Oversight**

- **Respecting Privacy:** As children grow older, they often seek more privacy and autonomy in their digital activities. Parents may struggle to find the right balance between respecting their children's independence and ensuring their safety online.
- **Inconsistent Rules and Boundaries:** Establishing consistent rules and boundaries for laptop and desktop use can be challenging, especially in households with multiple children of different ages. What is appropriate for a teenager may not be suitable for a younger sibling, leading to potential conflicts and confusion over device use.

Laptops and desktops are necessary tools for children, offering numerous benefits for education, creativity, and entertainment. However, they also present significant challenges and risks, from cybersecurity threats and privacy concerns to physical health issues and difficulties in parental supervision. By understanding these challenges, parents can better guide the complexities of their children's use of laptops and desktops, ensuring that these devices are used safely, responsibly, and in a way that supports their overall well-being.

3.4 Gaming Consoles

Gaming consoles have become a prominent part of many households, offering children and teenagers an exciting entertainment experience. From social interaction to educational games, gaming consoles provide a wide range of activities that can be both beneficial and potentially harmful. As these devices become more sophisticated, the challenges and risks associated with their use also increase, making it essential for parents to understand their impact on children's digital lives.

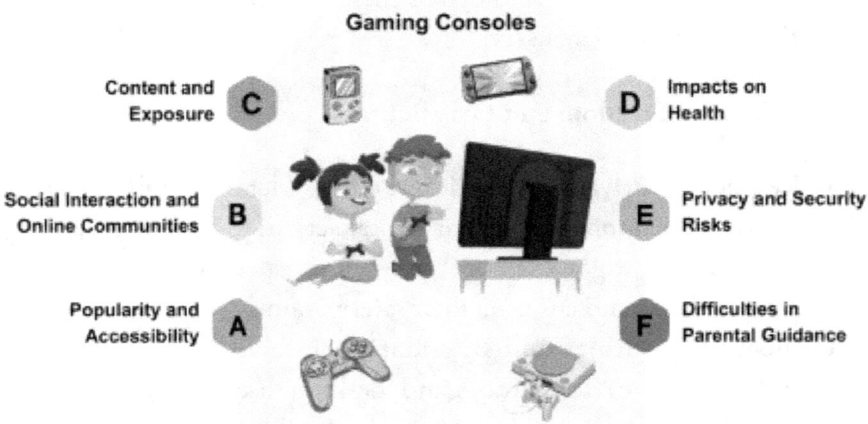

A) Popularity and Accessibility

1. Widespread Use

- **High Adoption Rates:** Gaming consoles such as the PlayStation, Xbox, and Nintendo Switch are highly popular among children and teenagers. Surveys show that approximately 83% of teens have access to a gaming console, making it one of the most common devices in this age group.

- **Age of Introduction:** Children are being introduced to gaming consoles at increasingly younger ages, often as early as 8 or 10 years old. This early exposure sets the stage for gaming becoming a regular part of their daily routine.

1. **Multi-functionality**

- **Beyond Gaming:** Modern gaming consoles are not just for playing video games. They also offer access to streaming services, social media, and even internet browsing. This multi-functionality means that gaming consoles can serve as a hub for various digital activities, expanding their influence on children's lives.
- **Portability:** Some gaming consoles, like the Nintendo Switch, offer portability, allowing children to play games on the go. This increases the time spent on gaming, as it can be done anywhere, from car rides to social gatherings.

B) Social Interaction and Online Communities

1. **Online Multiplayer Gaming**

- **Social Gaming:** One of the critical features of modern gaming consoles is the ability to connect with other players online. Games like Fortnite, Minecraft, and Call of Duty enable children to play with friends and strangers from around the world, creating virtual communities.
- **Voice and Text Chat:** Many games include voice and text chat features, allowing players to communicate in real time. While this can enhance the gaming experience, it also exposes children to risks such as cyberbullying, inappropriate language, and interaction with strangers.

1. **Pressure to Participate**

- **Peer Influence:** The social aspect of gaming consoles can create pressure for children to participate, especially when their friends are also playing. This can lead to excessive gaming as children strive to keep up with their peers, stay connected, and avoid feeling left out.

- **Competitive Environment:** Many online games are competitive, which can create stress and anxiety for children who feel the need to perform well. The desire to win or improve rankings can lead to frustration, mainly if the child is less skilled than others.

C) Content and Exposure

1. **Violent and Mature Content**

- **Inappropriate Games:** Gaming consoles offer access to a wide variety of games, some of which contain violent, explicit, or otherwise mature content that may not be suitable for children. Popular games often include themes of violence, aggression, and adult situations, which can influence a child's behavior and worldview.
- **Challenges in Filtering Content:** Although gaming consoles have parental controls that allow parents to restrict access to certain games or content, these settings are only sometimes reliable. Tech-savvy children may find ways to bypass these controls, gaining access to inappropriate material.

1. **In-Game Purchases and Micro-transactions**

- **Monetization Strategies:** Many console games include in-game purchases, such as buying skins, weapons, or other virtual goods. These microtransactions can quickly add up, leading to significant expenses. Children may not fully understand the financial implications of these purchases, which can result in unexpected charges on a parent's credit card.
- **Loot Boxes and Gambling:** Some games incorporate loot boxes—virtual items that contain random rewards—which have been criticized for mimicking gambling behavior. The excitement of opening loot boxes and the potential for rare items can encourage addictive behavior, particularly among younger players.

D) Impacts on Health

1. **Physical Health Implications**

- **Inactive Lifestyle:** Gaming consoles often encourage inactive behavior, as children spend extended periods sitting and playing games. This lack of physical activity can contribute to health issues such as obesity, poor cardiovascular health, and decreased muscle strength.
- **Eye Strain and Fatigue:** Long gaming sessions can lead to eye strain, headaches, and general fatigue, especially when children play in dimly lit environments or for hours on end without breaks.

1. **Mental Health Concerns**

- **Gaming Addiction:** The exciting and often addictive nature of video games can lead to gaming addiction. Children may become so lost in gaming that it interferes with their daily responsibilities, schoolwork, and social interactions. Symptoms of gaming addiction include an inability to stop playing, irritability when not gaming, and neglect of personal hygiene or sleep.
- **Emotional Impact:** The competitive nature of many games can lead to frustration, anger, and even aggressive behavior, particularly when children experience repeated losses or feel inadequate compared to their friends. The anonymity of online gaming can also lead to negative interactions that impact a child's self-esteem and emotional well-being.

E) Privacy and Security Risks

1. **Data Privacy Issues**

- **Personal Information Exposure:** Many gaming consoles require users to create online accounts that store personal information, including names, email addresses, and payment details. Children may unknowingly share this information with others, increasing the risk of identity theft or unauthorized access.

- **Third-Party Data Sharing:** Some games and platforms may collect data on player's habits, preferences, and interactions, which can be shared with third parties for advertising or other purposes. This can lead to targeted ads or other privacy concerns that parents may not be aware of.

1. **Vulnerability to Online Predators**

- **Risk of Grooming**: The social aspect of online gaming can expose children to online predators who may use gaming platforms to initiate contact. These individuals might attempt to groom children by building trust, sharing personal information, and eventually leading the child into dangerous situations.
- **Challenges in Monitoring:** Given the interactive and real-time nature of online gaming, it can be challenging for parents to monitor all interactions their child has with others. Conversations and exchanges can happen quickly, often leaving little trace, making it difficult for parents to detect harmful behavior.

F) Difficulties in Parental Guidance

1. **Difficulty in Monitoring Usage**

- **Private Gaming Spaces:** Gaming consoles are often used in private spaces, such as a child's bedroom, making it difficult for parents to monitor what games are being played and how much time is being spent on the console. This lack of oversight can lead to concerns about the content being consumed and the behaviors being encouraged.
- **Complexity of Parental Controls:** While gaming consoles offer parental control features, setting them up can be complex and time-consuming. Additionally, tech-savvy children may find ways to bypass these controls, further complicating parental efforts to manage their child's gaming habits.

1. **Balancing Gaming with Other Activities**

- **Establishing Limits:** One of the biggest challenges for parents is establishing and enforcing limits on gaming time. Children may resist these limits, especially if they feel that their gaming time is being unfairly restricted compared to their peers. Balancing gaming with other essential activities, such as homework, physical exercise, and family time, can be difficult.
- **Inconsistent Rules:** Setting consistent rules for gaming console use can be challenging in households with multiple children, mainly when children are of different ages and have varying levels of maturity. What is appropriate for an older child may not be suitable for a younger sibling, leading to potential conflicts and confusion.

Gaming consoles provide children with a rich and engaging entertainment experience, but they also come with significant risks and challenges. From exposure to violent content and the potential for gaming addiction to privacy concerns and difficulties in parental supervision, these devices require careful management. By understanding these challenges, parents can better navigate the complexities of gaming console use, helping their children enjoy the benefits while minimizing the risks.

3.5 Smart TVs and Other Connected Devices

Smart TVs and other connected devices, such as streaming sticks, smart speakers, and internet-connected toys, have become increasingly common in households, offering children remarkable access to a vast collection of content and interactive experiences. While these devices can enhance entertainment and learning, they also introduce new challenges and risks that parents must point out to ensure their children's safety and well-being in the digital world.

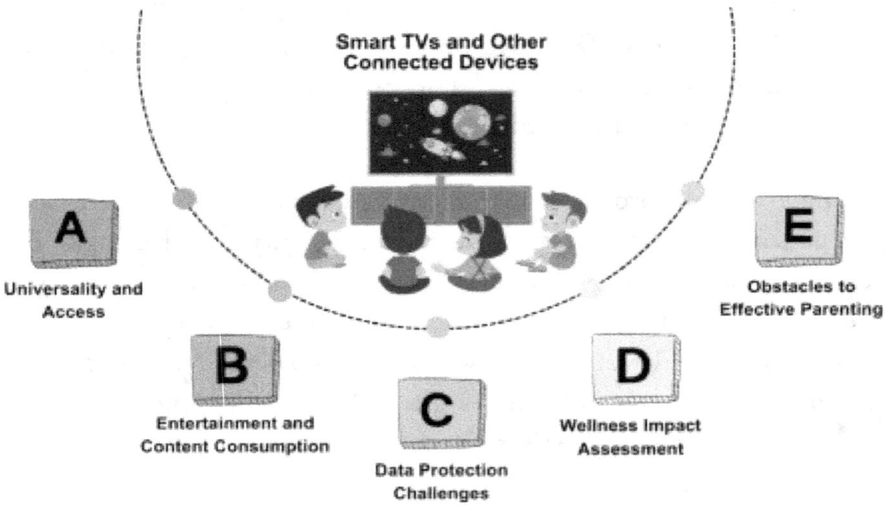

A) Universality and Access

1. **Widespread Adoption of Smart TVs**

- **Prevalence in Households:** Smart TVs are now a standard feature in many homes, allowing families to stream content directly from the internet without the need for additional devices. These TVs provide easy access to platforms like Netflix, YouTube, and Disney+, making them a central hub for family entertainment.
- **Ease of Use for Children:** Smart TVs are designed with user-friendly interfaces that are easy for children to navigate. Many smart TVs come with voice-activated controls, which allow even younger children to

search for and play their favorite shows and movies independently.

1. **Integration with Other Connected Devices**

- **Streaming Sticks and Boxes:** Devices like Amazon Fire Stick, Roku, and Apple TV can turn any regular TV into a smart TV, providing access to streaming services, apps, and games. Children often use these devices to watch content, play games, or even browse the internet.
- **Smart Speakers and Assistants:** Devices like Amazon Echo, Google Home, and Apple HomePod have become popular in many households. These smart speakers, equipped with virtual assistants, allow children to ask questions, play music, or control other connected devices with simple voice commands.

B) Entertainment and Content Consumption

1. **Access to a Wide Range of Content**

- **Streaming Services:** Smart TVs and connected devices offer access to a broad spectrum of streaming services, including those specifically designed for children, such as YouTube Kids and Disney+. However, they also provide access to content that may need to be age-appropriate, leading to concerns about what children are watching.
- **Interactive Content:** Some smart TVs and connected devices offer interactive content, such as educational games or shows that require viewer participation. While this can be an engaging way to learn, it also blurs the line between entertainment and interactive media, potentially leading to longer screen time.

1. **Challenges in Content Filtering**

- **Difficulty in Monitoring:** The wide range of content available on smart TVs and connected devices can make it difficult for parents to monitor what their children are watching. Unlike traditional TV, where content is scheduled, streaming services allow children to access a vast library of on-demand content, which can include material that is inappropriate for their age.

- **Advertisements and In-App Purchases:** Many free apps and streaming services available on smart TVs and connected devices are supported by advertisements or offer in-app purchases. These can expose children to targeted ads or lead to unintentional purchases, creating financial and ethical concerns.

C) Data Protection Challenges

1. Data Collection and Privacy Issues

- **Tracking and Data Sharing:** Smart TVs and connected devices often collect data on user preferences, viewing habits, and interactions. This data is sometimes shared with third parties for advertising and other purposes, raising concerns about privacy. Children, who may not understand the implications of data collection, are particularly vulnerable to these practices.
- **Voice-Activated Devices:** Smart speakers and other voice-activated devices are always listening for commands, which means they are continuously collecting audio data. While this technology is convenient, it also raises concerns about who has access to this data and how it is being used.

1. Vulnerability to Hacking

- **Security Risks:** Like any internet-connected device, smart TVs and connected devices are vulnerable to hacking. Hackers can gain access to these devices to spy on users, steal personal information, or manipulate the content being displayed. This risk is particularly concerning when children are using these devices unsupervised.
- **Insecure Connected Toys:** Internet-connected toys that interact with children, such as those that use Bluetooth or Wi-Fi, can also pose security risks. If these toys are not properly secured, they can be hacked, leading to privacy breaches or inappropriate interactions.

D) Wellness Impact Assessment

1. Physical Health Concerns

- **Increased Screen Time:** The ease of access to a vast array of content on smart TVs and connected devices can lead to increased screen time for children. Lengthy screen time is associated with various health issues, including eye strain, sleep disruption, and decreased physical activity.
- **Sedentary Behavior:** The passive nature of watching TV or using connected devices often encourages inactive behavior. Children who spend long periods in front of screens may miss out on physical activities that are crucial for their health and development.

1. Mental Health Considerations

- **Content Influence on Behavior:** The content children consume on smart TVs, and connected devices can influence their behavior, attitudes, and perceptions. Exposure to violent or inappropriate content can lead to aggressive behavior, fear, or confusion, particularly in younger children.
- **Impact on Sleep Patterns:** The use of smart TVs and connected devices, especially before bedtime, can interfere with children's sleep patterns. The blue light emitted by screens can disrupt the production of melatonin, leading to difficulties falling asleep and reduced sleep quality.

E) Obstacles to Effective Parenting

1. Monitoring and Controlling Access

- **Complexity of Parental Controls:** While many smart TVs and connected devices offer parental control features, these can be complex to set up and manage. Parents may need help to configure these settings effectively, especially if they are not familiar with the technology.

- **Multi-Device Environment:** In households with multiple connected devices, it can be challenging for parents to monitor and control what their children are accessing. Children may move from one device to another, making it difficult to track their screen time and the content they are consuming.

1. **Balancing Entertainment and Education**

- **Educational and Recreational Use:** Parents often face the challenge of balancing educational content with recreational use. While smart TVs and connected devices can be valuable tools for learning, they are also sources of endless entertainment, which can be distracting and lead to overconsumption.
- **Encouraging Healthy Habits:** Establishing and enforcing rules around the use of smart TVs and connected devices can be difficult, mainly when these devices are a central part of family entertainment. Encouraging children to take breaks, engage in physical activity, and prioritize other activities over screen time is essential for maintaining a healthy balance.

Smart TVs and other connected devices offer children access to a vast array of content and interactive experiences, enhancing both entertainment and learning opportunities. However, these devices also present significant challenges and risks, including privacy concerns, exposure to inappropriate content, and increased screen time. Understanding these challenges is crucial for parents who want to navigate the complexities of connected devices in their children's lives. By being aware of the potential risks and implementing effective strategies for monitoring and control, parents can help ensure that their children use these devices safely and responsibly.

3.6 Wearable Technology and the Internet of Things (IoT)

Wearable technology and the Internet of Things (IoT) have introduced a new dimension to how children interact with the digital world. Devices like smartwatches, fitness trackers, and internet-connected toys are becoming increasingly popular among kids, offering a blend of convenience, entertainment, and learning opportunities. However, these advancements also bring unique challenges and risks that parents need to be aware of to ensure their children's safety in the connected world.

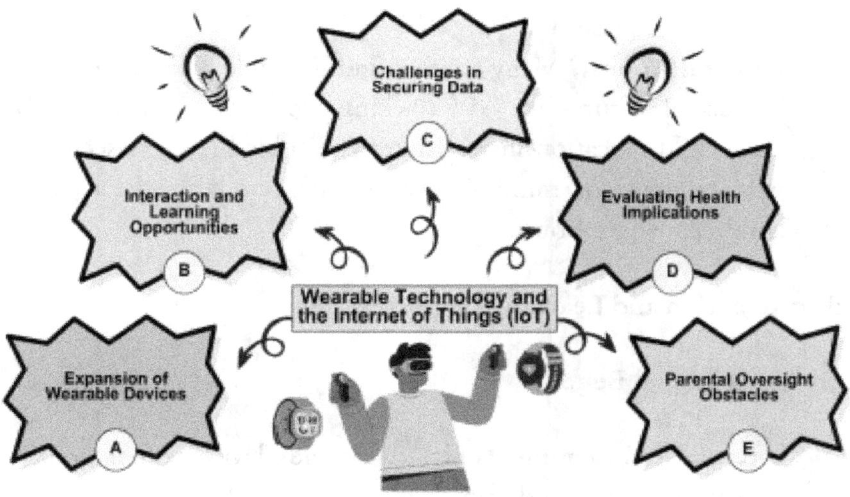

A) Expansion of Wearable Devices

1. Growing Popularity among Kids

- **Smartwatches and Fitness Trackers**: Devices like smartwatches and fitness trackers are increasingly popular among children. They are often marketed as tools for health monitoring and communication. These wearables allow kids to track their physical activity, monitor their health, and even communicate with parents through calls and messages.

- **Internet-Connected Toys:** Toys embedded with IoT technology, such as interactive dolls or robots, are designed to provide a captivating experience for children. These toys can connect to the internet to access additional content, learn new behaviors, or interact with other connected devices.

1. **Convenience and Everyday Use**

- **Ease of Integration:** Wearable devices are designed to be worn throughout the day, seamlessly integrating into a child's daily routine. Smartwatches can be used to tell time, set reminders, and even play games, while fitness trackers encourage physical activity by tracking steps and exercise.
- **Parental Appeal:** Many parents find wearable technology appealing because of features like GPS tracking, which allows them to monitor their child's location in real time. This added layer of security gives parents peace of mind, knowing they can keep checks on their children's whereabouts.

B) Interaction and Learning Opportunities

1. **Educational Benefits**

- **Interactive Learning Tools:** Wearable devices often come with educational apps and games that promote learning in a fun and interactive way. For example, smartwatches may include spelling games, math challenges, or language learning tools that help children build essential skills while playing.
- **Health and Fitness Education:** Fitness trackers are designed to teach children about the importance of physical activity and healthy habits. By setting goals and tracking progress, children can learn about fitness and wellness in an engaging and motivating way.

1. **Encouragement of Healthy Habits**

- **Physical Activity Promotion:** Many wearables encourage children to be more active by setting daily step goals, tracking their movement, and providing rewards for achieving fitness milestones. This can be particularly beneficial in combating sedentary lifestyles and promoting overall health.

- **Sleep Monitoring:** Some wearable devices come with sleep-tracking features that monitor a child's sleep patterns. These features help parents identify issues such as insufficient rest or irregular sleep cycles. This data can be helpful in promoting better sleep hygiene and improving a child's overall well-being.

C) Challenges in Securing Data

1. **Data Collection and Privacy Risks**

- **Personal Data Monitoring:** Wearable devices collect a significant amount of personal data, including location, health metrics, and usage patterns. This information can be sensitive, especially when it involves children, and there are concerns about how companies store, share, and use it.
- **Location Tracking:** While GPS tracking can be helpful for parents, it also raises privacy concerns. Constantly tracking a child's location can lead to potential misuse of this data if it falls into the wrong hands. Moreover, children may not fully understand the implications of being constantly monitored.

1. **Vulnerability to Hacking**

- **Security Weaknesses:** Many wearable devices, particularly those designed for children, have been found to have security vulnerabilities that hackers could exploit. These weaknesses can lead to unauthorized access to the device, allowing hackers to track a child's location, intercept communications, or gain access to personal data.
- **Insecure IoT Ecosystems:** The interconnected nature of IoT devices means that if one device is compromised, it could potentially provide a gateway to other connected devices in the home. This

interconnectedness amplifies the risk of a security breach, making it essential for parents to understand the security features of each device.

D) Evaluating Health Implications

1. Physical Health Implications

- **Radiation Exposure:** Some parents express concerns about the potential health risks associated with the radiation emitted by wearable devices, particularly those that use Bluetooth or Wi-Fi for connectivity. While research on the long-term effects of radiation exposure from wearables is still ongoing, parents need to be aware of these concerns.
- **Comfort and Durability:** Wearable devices are designed to be worn for extended periods, which means they need to be comfortable and durable. However, children may experience discomfort from wearing these devices for long hours, or the devices may cause skin irritation or allergic reactions.

1. Impact on Mental Well-Being

- **Over-Reliance on Devices:** As with any technology, there is a risk that children may become overly reliant on wearable devices, leading to an unhealthy attachment. For example, children may become anxious if they are separated from their smartwatch or feel pressured to meet the goals set by their fitness tracker.
- **Sleep Disruption:** Some wearable devices are designed to monitor sleep patterns while worn during sleep. However, wearing a device at night could potentially disrupt a child's sleep, mainly if the device emits light or vibrates during the night.

E) Parental Oversight Obstacles

1. Monitoring and Controlling Use

- **Complexity of Device Management:** Wearable devices often come with their own set of apps and settings that parents need to manage. Keeping track of these settings, such as privacy controls and app permissions, can be challenging, primarily when children use multiple devices.

- **Balancing Benefits and Risks:** Parents need to strike a balance between the benefits of wearable technology—such as increased security and educational opportunities—and the risks, including privacy concerns and potential over-reliance on technology.

1. **Awareness of Potential Risks**

- **Lack of Transparency:** Not all wearable devices provide transparent information about their data collection practices, security features, or potential health risks. Parents may need help finding reliable information about the devices their children are using, making it difficult to make informed decisions.
- **Educating Children about Risks:** Parents need to educate their children about the potential risks associated with wearable technology. This includes understanding the importance of not sharing personal information, being aware of the device's limitations, and recognizing when it is appropriate to take a break from using the device.

Wearable technology and IoT devices offer exciting new opportunities for children to learn, stay active, and remain connected. However, these benefits come with a range of challenges and risks, particularly in terms of privacy, security, and health. As these devices become more integrated into daily life, parents must stay informed about the potential implications for their children. By understanding the risks and implementing appropriate safeguards, parents can help ensure that their children use wearable technology and IoT devices safely and responsibly. The devices that children use to access the internet—ranging from smartphones and tablets to gaming consoles, smart TVs, and wearable technology—offer incredible opportunities for learning, entertainment, and communication. However, these devices also introduce significant challenges and risks, from privacy concerns and exposure to inappropriate content to the potential for physical and mental health issues. Understanding these challenges is the first step toward ensuring that our children navigate the digital world safely. In the next chapter, we will discuss deeper about these challenges and risks, exploring how they impact children's digital lives and what parents can do to address them effectively.

Chapter 4: Potential Online Threats and Dangers

As our children continue to explore the vast digital landscape, they encounter numerous opportunities for learning, social interaction, and entertainment. However, alongside these benefits lie significant threats and dangers that can have a profound impact on their safety, privacy, and overall well-being. In this chapter, we will look into the most pressing online risks that children face today, providing parents with a comprehensive understanding of the digital hazards that require careful attention.

Cyberbullying

The internet is not just a space for knowledge and connection; it is also a domain where harmful activities can quickly occur. Cyberbullying is a prime example, where harassment and bullying surpass physical boundaries and infiltrate the very devices children use for communication and learning. This form of bullying can be relentless, leading to severe emotional and psychological consequences that are difficult to escape.

Exposure to Inappropriate Content

Another pressing concern is the exposure to inappropriate content. With just a few clicks, children can unintentionally access material that is violent, explicit, or otherwise unsuitable for their age. The vastness of the internet makes it nearly impossible to shield young minds from all harmful content, raising significant challenges for parents.

Online Predators

Online predators pose a particularly deceptive threat. These individuals exploit the anonymity of the internet to groom and manipulate children, often using social media, gaming platforms, or chat rooms to establish contact. The dangers posed by such predators are both real and alarming, requiring vigilant awareness from parents to protect their children from exploitation.

Privacy Risks and Data Security

In addition to these interpersonal threats, the digital world also carries privacy risks and data security issues. Children, often unaware of the importance of protecting personal information, may accidentally share sensitive details online, making them targets for identity theft, fraud, and other forms of exploitation. The misuse of personal data can have long-lasting consequences, making it a critical area of concern.

Addiction and Overuse

Moreover, the internet is full of opportunities for addiction and overuse. The engaging nature of social media, games, and streaming services can lead to excessive screen time, which not only affects physical health but also contributes to mental health issues such as anxiety and depression. Understanding the addictive elements of these platforms is crucial for helping children maintain a balanced digital life.

Phishing and Online Scams

Another significant danger comes from phishing and online scams. These deceptive tactics are designed to trick individuals into revealing personal information or installing malicious software. Children, with their limited understanding of online security, are particularly vulnerable to such schemes, which can result in financial loss or compromised security.

Malware and Viruses

Finally, the threat of malware and viruses largely endangers the digital environment. These malicious programs can infect devices, leading to data loss, privacy breaches, and even identity theft. Children may unknowingly download such harmful software, highlighting the importance of vital cybersecurity practices in the household.

This chapter will explore each of these threats in detail, explaining how they manifest, why they are concerning, and the potential impact they can have on children's lives. By understanding these dangers, parents can better equip themselves to protect their children in the digital world. While these threats are serious, knowledge and awareness are the first steps toward ensuring a safer online experience for our children.

4.1 Cyberbullying

Cyberbullying is one of the most widespread and damaging threats that children face in the digital world. Unlike traditional bullying, which is confined to physical spaces like schools or playgrounds, cyberbullying can follow children everywhere—into their homes, onto their devices, and into their most private moments. This form of bullying leverages the anonymity and reach of the internet to harass, threaten, or humiliate victims, often with devastating emotional and psychological effects.

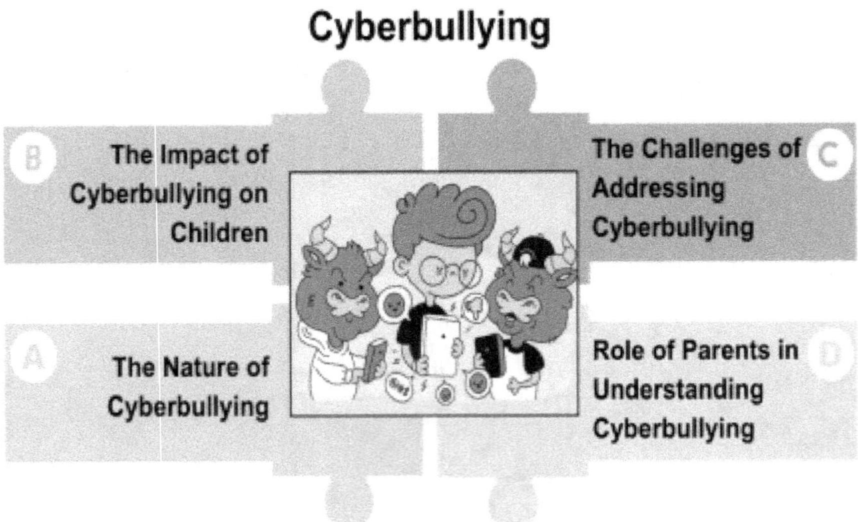

A) The Nature of Cyberbullying

1. **What Is Cyberbullying?**

- **Definition and Forms:** Cyberbullying refers to the use of digital platforms—such as social media, messaging apps, online forums, and gaming platforms—to engage in behaviors that are intended to harm, intimidate, or belittle another person. This can include spreading rumors, posting hurtful comments, sharing private information without consent, or creating fake profiles to deceive and manipulate others.

- **Perpetrators and Victims:** Cyberbullying can be committed by friends, acquaintances, or even strangers. Often, the anonymity provided by the internet encourages bullies, allowing them to act without the fear of immediate consequences. Victims of cyberbullying can be targeted for a variety of reasons, including their appearance, social status, race, gender, or beliefs.

1. **The Digital Reach**

- **24/7 Exposure:** Unlike traditional bullying, which typically occurs during specific times and in certain locations, cyberbullying can happen at any time and in any place. The widespread nature of digital communication means that children can be targeted while they are at home, on vacation, or even during the middle of the night. This constant exposure can leave victims feeling trapped, with no safe space to escape the harassment.
- **Viral Spread:** One of the most alarming aspects of cyberbullying is its potential to go viral. A hurtful message, embarrassing photo, or damaging rumor can be shared and reshared across multiple platforms, quickly reaching a broad audience. This can amplify the impact of the bullying, as the victim is not only harassed by the original wrongdoer but also by those who participate in the spread of the content.

B) The Impact of Cyberbullying on Children

1. **Emotional and Psychological Effects**

- **Anxiety and Depression:** Children who are victims of cyberbullying often experience significant emotional distress. The relentless nature of online harassment can lead to feelings of anxiety, depression, and helplessness. Many victims struggle with the fear of being constantly judged or attacked, which can severely impact their mental health.
- **Low Self-Esteem and Isolation:** Cyberbullying can erode a child's self-esteem, making them feel worthless, unloved, and isolated. The

public nature of online platforms means that bullying incidents are often witnessed by others, which can intensify the victim's feelings of shame and humiliation. In extreme cases, this can lead to social withdrawal, where the child avoids interactions both online and offline.

1. **Academic and Social Consequences**

- **Decline in Academic Performance:** The stress and anxiety caused by cyberbullying can interfere with a child's ability to focus on their studies. Victims may experience a decline in academic performance, skip classes to avoid further harassment, or even drop out of school entirely.
- **Social Relationships:** Cyberbullying can also damage a child's social relationships. Victims may struggle to trust others, leading to difficulties in forming and maintaining friendships. In some cases, they may become targets of exclusion, where peers distance themselves for fear of becoming associated with the victim.

C) The Challenges of Addressing Cyberbullying

1. **Anonymity and Detection**

- **Anonymity of Perpetrators:** One of the most challenging aspects of addressing cyberbullying is the anonymity that the internet provides. Bullies can hide behind fake profiles or use apps that mask their identity, making it challenging to identify and confront them. This anonymity can also encourage bullies to be more aggressive and relentless in their attacks.
- **Difficulty in Detection:** Unlike traditional bullying, which is often visible to teachers or parents, cyberbullying can be hidden behind the screens of personal devices. Children may not report incidents of cyberbullying out of fear of retaliation, embarrassment, or the belief that nothing can be done to stop it. This makes it challenging for parents and educators to detect and intervene in cases of

cyberbullying.

1. **Legal and Platform Challenges**

- **Inconsistent Legal Protections:** While many countries have laws that address cyberbullying, the enforcement of these laws can be inconsistent. The digital nature of cyberbullying means that incidents can cross jurisdictional boundaries, complicating efforts to hold offenders accountable. Additionally, the legal definitions of cyberbullying can vary, making it difficult to pursue justice in some cases.
- **Platform Response:** Social media platforms and other digital services often have policies against cyberbullying, but the enforcement of these policies can be inconsistent. Reporting mechanisms may only sometimes lead to timely or practical action, and in some cases, the content may remain online despite repeated reports. This can make it difficult for victims to find relief and protection from ongoing harassment.

D) The Role of Parents in Understanding Cyberbullying

1. **Awareness and Education**

- **Understanding the Threat:** Parents need to be aware of the risks and signs of cyberbullying to protect their children effectively. This involves educating themselves about the platforms their children use, the types of interactions that can occur online, and the potential impact of cyberbullying on their child's well-being.
- **Open Communication:** Establishing open lines of communication with children is crucial in addressing cyberbullying. Children who feel comfortable talking to their parents about their online experiences are more likely to report incidents of cyberbullying and seek support when needed.

1. **Monitoring and Support**

- **Monitoring Online Activity:** While respecting a child's privacy is important, parents also need to find ways to monitor their child's online activity to detect signs of cyberbullying. This can include checking in on social media accounts, reviewing messages, and being alert to changes in behavior that may indicate something is wrong.
- **Emotional Support:** It is essential to provide emotional support to a child who is experiencing cyberbullying. Parents should offer reassurance, listen without judgment, and work together with their child to find solutions, whether that involves reporting bullying, seeking help from school officials, or accessing professional counselling.

Cyberbullying is a complex and widespread threat that can have devastating effects on a child's emotional, psychological, and social well-being. The anonymity and reach of the internet make it a particularly misleading form of harassment, one that can follow children wherever they go. As parents, understanding the nature of cyberbullying and its impact is crucial for protecting children in the digital world. While addressing cyberbullying presents significant challenges, awareness and proactive involvement are vital to ensuring that children can navigate the internet safely and confidently.

What can parents do if bullying occurs?

1. Listen to the child without judging. An environment where the child feels free to speak, is heard, and feels comfortable. Being supportive is really important as a first step in handling cyberbullying.
2. It's Important to stay calm and composed. As parent's when they hear about such incidents from their children, it's natural for them to react, but it's important to handle emotions well to let the kids know that they can trust their parents to handle such situations.
3. Document everything you can. Screenshots, witnesses, date, time, location. The sooner you do this, the better.
4. Do not engage with the bully. Block and report to the online platform.
5. If this is someone from the school make sure the school is aware of this. Share all the information so that the incident is documented within the school records.

6. Seek a counsellor if it impacts the mental health of the child.
7. Teach children that it is not them. The goal is not to block online platform access for them but to be aware of cyberbullying and build resilience and safe online habits that will help them detect such incidents and protect them in the long term.

4.2 Exposure to Inappropriate Content

In the vast and unregulated expanse of the internet, children are constantly at risk of encountering content that is inappropriate for their age and development. The digital world's accessibility and anonymity mean that, with just a few clicks, young users can be exposed to material that can be disturbing, confusing, or harmful. This exposure is one of the most significant challenges parents face in protecting their children online, as inappropriate content can significantly affect a child's emotional, psychological, and moral development.

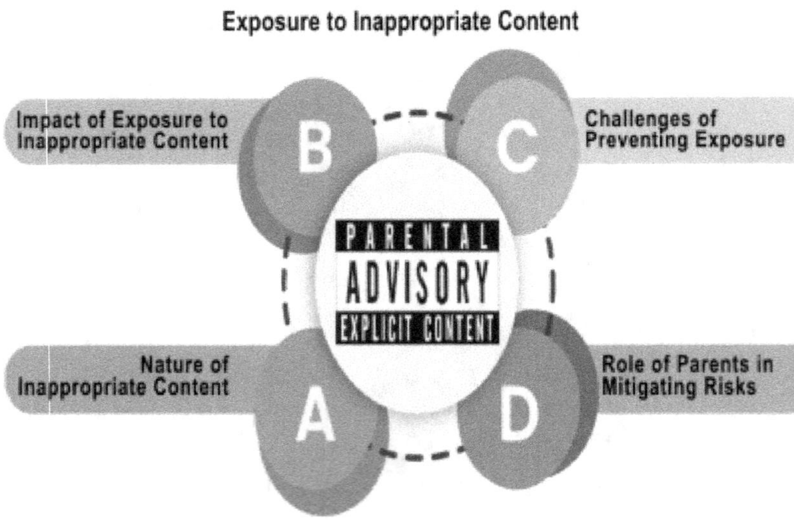

A) The Nature of Inappropriate Content

1. **What Constitutes Inappropriate Content?**

- **Violent Content:** One of the most prominent forms of inappropriate content children may encounter online is violence. This includes graphic images or videos depicting physical harm, abuse, or death. Exposure to such content can expose children to violence, distort their understanding of conflict resolution, and induce fear or anxiety.
- **Sexually Explicit Material:** The internet is filled with sexually explicit

material, including pornography, which is easily accessible and often shared without filters. Exposure to such content can have a lasting impact on a child's understanding of relationships, sexuality, and consent, potentially leading to unhealthy attitudes and behaviors.

- **Hate Speech and Extremism:** Children may also encounter content that promotes hate speech, racism, sexism, or other forms of discrimination. Such material can influence a child's beliefs and values, promoting intolerance and hostility towards others.
- **Substance Abuse and Self-Harm:** There is also content that promotes substance abuse, self-harm, or other dangerous behaviors. This type of content can be particularly harmful as it may encourage fraud or normalize these behaviors in the eyes of persuadable children.

1. **How Children Encounter Inappropriate Content**

- **Accidental Exposure:** Children often encounter inappropriate content accidentally while searching for something else or through seemingly innocent links or pop-ups on social media platforms, video streaming sites, or even educational websites that are not adequately filtered.
- **Peer Sharing:** Children may also be exposed to inappropriate content through their peers, who might share links or videos in group chats, during online gaming sessions, or through social media. Peer pressure can sometimes lead children to view content they would otherwise avoid.
- **Curiosity and Exploration:** As children grow older, their natural curiosity about the world may lead them to explore content that is not suitable for their age. This curiosity can drive them to seek out information about topics like sex, violence, or adult activities, which can expose them to harmful material.

B) The Impact of Exposure to Inappropriate Content

1. **Emotional and Psychological Effects**

- **Fear and Anxiety:** Exposure to violent or disturbing content can instil fear and anxiety in children. They may have nightmares, develop irrational fears, or become overly anxious about their safety and the safety of those around them.
- **Confusion and Distress:** Inappropriate content, particularly sexually explicit material, can cause confusion and distress. Children may struggle to understand what they have seen and may feel shame or guilt, especially if they sense that the content is forbidden or not meant for them.
- **Desensitization:** Repeated exposure to violent or explicit content can lead to desensitization, where children become impassive to the severity of such material. This can result in a lack of empathy, increased aggression, or an unhealthy acceptance of violence or sexual exploitation as normal behavior.

1. **Moral and Social Development**

- **Distorted Values:** Inappropriate content can significantly impact a child's developing sense of right and wrong. For example, exposure to hate speech or extremist ideologies can shape a child's beliefs in harmful ways, leading them to adopt intolerant or violent attitudes.
- **Impacts on Relationships:** Exposure to sexually explicit content can affect how children view relationships and intimacy. It can lead to unrealistic expectations about sex, a lack of understanding about consent, or the objectification of others, all of which can have negative implications for their future relationships.

C) The Challenges of Preventing Exposure

1. **Unregulated Content Platforms**

- **Lack of Effective Filters:** Many platforms that children use, such as video-sharing websites and social media, need more effective filters to prevent exposure to inappropriate content. Even when parental controls are in place, children may still encounter harmful material due to the sheer volume of content uploaded daily.

- **User-Generated Content:** The wide range of user-generated material, which is frequently subject to different inspection or regulation than professional media, makes regulating exposure to improper content a considerable concern. This content can range from seemingly harmless videos with hidden inappropriate elements to direct uploads of explicit material.

1. **Inadequate Parental Controls**

- **Complexity and Limitations:** Parental control tools are often complex to set up and manage, and they may only cover some of the platforms or devices that children use. Additionally, tech-savvy children may find ways to bypass these controls, making it difficult for parents to protect them fully from exposure to harmful content.
- **Inconsistent Application Across Devices:** Children access the internet from multiple devices—smartphones, tablets, laptops, and gaming consoles—so ensuring that parental controls are consistently applied across all platforms is challenging. Each device may require different settings, and parents may not be aware of all the content their child can access.

1. **Peer Influence and Social Norms**

- **Peer Pressure:** Even if a child's digital environment is well-controlled, they can still be exposed to inappropriate content through friends and relatives. Peer pressure can play a significant role in this, as children may feel driven to view or share content to fit in with their friends or to avoid being teased.
- **Normalization of Inappropriate Content:** In some online communities, particularly among older children and teenagers, certain types of inappropriate content may be normalized or even celebrated. This can make it more difficult for children to recognize the material as harmful or to resist engaging with it.

D) The Role of Parents in Mitigating Risks

1. **Awareness and Vigilance**

- **Understanding the Risks:** Parents need to be aware of the types of inappropriate content their children might encounter and the platforms where such content is most likely to appear. This awareness is crucial for setting appropriate boundaries and monitoring online activity.
- **Regular Monitoring:** Regularly monitoring a child's internet usage, including the websites they visit and the content they engage with, is essential for identifying potential risks early on. This can involve checking browser histories, using parental control software, and discussing their online activities openly.

1. **Open Communication**

- **Talking About Content:** Open communication is vital in helping children navigate the digital world safely. Parents should create an environment where children feel comfortable discussing what they see online, including any content that makes them uncomfortable or confused. These discussions can help children understand why certain content is inappropriate and how to avoid it.
- **Setting Clear Guidelines:** Establishing clear guidelines about what is acceptable to view online and the consequences of accessing inappropriate content can help children make better decisions. These guidelines should be age-appropriate and regularly reviewed as the child grows and their digital habits evolve.

Exposure to inappropriate content is a significant threat that can have lasting effects on a child's emotional, psychological, and moral development. In the unregulated and expansive world of the internet, protecting children from harmful material is a complex but essential task for parents. By understanding the nature of inappropriate content, the ways children may encounter it, and the impact it can have, parents can take proactive steps to mitigate these risks.

Through vigilance, open communication, and the use of adequate parental controls, parents can help guide their children toward a safer and more positive online experience.

4.3 Online Predators

The digital world offers outstanding opportunities for connection and communication, but it also presents significant risks, particularly when it comes to the threat of online predators. These individuals exploit the anonymity and accessibility of the internet to target, manipulate, and exploit children. Online predators can be found on social media platforms, gaming sites, chat rooms, and other digital spaces where children are likely to interact. Understanding the tactics these predators use and the dangers they pose is crucial for parents who want to protect their children in the digital age.

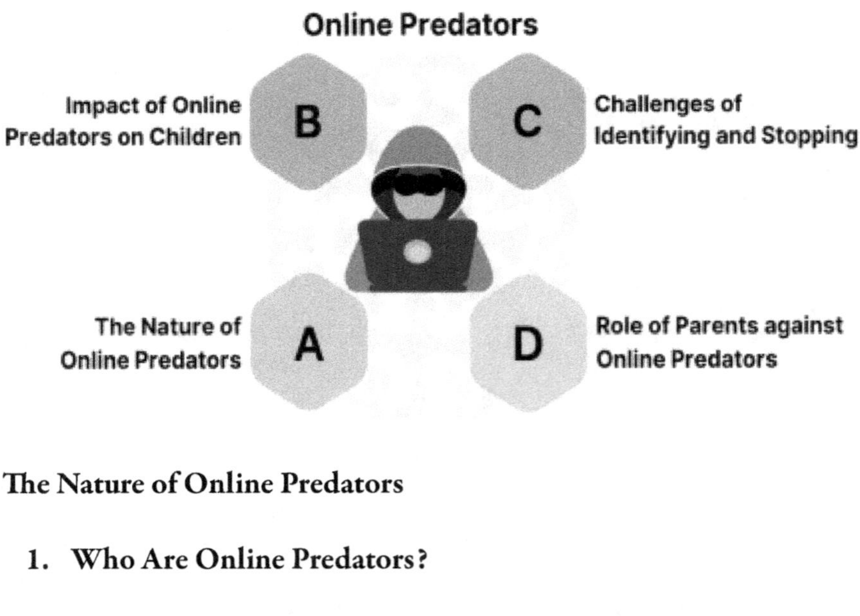

A) The Nature of Online Predators

1. **Who Are Online Predators?**

- **Definition and Characteristics:** Online predators are individuals who use the internet to exploit children, often for sexual purposes. They may pose as children or teenagers to gain the trust of their victims, using false identities and fabricated stories to create a sense of connection. These predators are skilled at manipulating their targets, gradually gaining their trust before attempting to exploit them.
- **Types of Predators:** Online predators can vary in their methods and intentions. Some seek to establish inappropriate relationships with

children, while others may aim to exploit them through the sharing of explicit content or even human trafficking. The common thread among these predators is their desire to take advantage of a child's vulnerability and childishness.

1. How Predators Operate

- **Grooming Process:** One of the primary tactics used by online predators is grooming, a gradual process of building trust and emotional connection with a child. This process often begins with innocent conversations and compliments, which evolve into more personal and intimate exchanges. The predator may use overpraise, attention, and gifts to make the child feel unique and valued, all while encouraging them to keep the relationship secret from parents and other authority figures.
- **Exploiting Vulnerabilities:** Predators often target children who are lonely, insecure, or experiencing difficulties at home or school. They exploit these vulnerabilities by offering support, understanding, and validation, positioning themselves as the child's confidant. Once trust is established, the predator may begin to introduce sexual content or request explicit photos, often framing these requests as a natural progression of their "relationship."
- **Isolation and Control:** As the grooming process progresses, the predator may attempt to isolate the child from their friends and family, creating a sense of dependence on the relationship. They may also use threats, guilt, or emotional manipulation to maintain control over the child and prevent them from seeking help.

B) The Impact of Online Predators on Children

1. Emotional and Psychological Effects

- **Fear and Anxiety:** Children who online predators target often experience significant fear and anxiety. They may feel trapped in the situation, afraid to speak out due to threats or the fear of not being believed. This can lead to a deep sense of isolation as the child struggles to cope with the emotional burden on their own.

- **Guilt and Shame:** Predators often manipulate their victims into believing that they are to blame for the situation. This can result in intense feelings of guilt and shame, which may prevent the child from seeking help or disclosing what has happened. The psychological damage caused by these emotions can have long-lasting effects, potentially leading to depression, self-harm, or other mental health issues.

1. **Long-Term Consequences**

- **Loss of Trust:** Children who online predators have targeted may develop a deep mistrust of others, particularly adults. This can affect their ability to form healthy relationships in the future, as they struggle with feelings of betrayal and a fear of being taken advantage of again.
- **Trauma and PTSD:** The experiences that result from online predation can be deeply traumatic. Children who have been exploited may have post-traumatic stress disorder (PTSD), characterized by flashbacks, nightmares, and severe anxiety. The trauma can impact their academic performance, social interactions, and overall well-being, potentially requiring long-term psychological support to heal.

C) The Challenges of Identifying and Stopping Online Predators

1. **Anonymity and Deception**

- **False Identities:** The internet allows predators to easily create false identities, making it difficult for children and parents to identify potential threats. Predators may use fake profiles, altered photos, and fabricated personal details to convince children that they are someone they are not. This anonymity makes it challenging to track and arrest these individuals.
- **Complex Networks:** Many predators are part of more extensive,

organized networks that share tactics, strategies, and even victims. These networks can be highly sophisticated, using encrypted communication methods and dark web platforms to avoid detection by law enforcement. The complexity of these networks adds a layer of difficulty in identifying and stopping online predators.

1. **Delayed Detection**

- **Hidden Grooming Tactics:** The grooming process is often hidden and drawn out, making it difficult for parents or other adults to detect what is happening. Predators are skilled at hiding their intentions until they have fully gained the child's trust, by which time significant damage may already have been done.
- **Lack of Reporting:** Many children do not report their interactions with online predators due to fear, shame, or confusion about what is happening. This lack of reporting can allow predators to continue their activities undetected, putting more children at risk.

D) The Role of Parents in Protecting Children from Online Predators

1. **Awareness and Vigilance**

- **Understanding the Threat:** Parents must be aware of the threat posed by online predators and the tactics they use to target children. This awareness includes understanding the platforms and apps where predators are most likely to operate and recognizing the signs of grooming.
- **Monitoring Online Activity:** Regularly monitoring a child's online activity is crucial in detecting potential interactions with predators. This includes checking social media profiles, reviewing chat logs, and being alert to any secretive behavior or sudden changes in the child's mood or behavior.

1. **Open Communication**

- **Encouraging Openness:** Creating an environment where children feel comfortable discussing their online experiences is vital in protecting them from predators. Parents should encourage their children to talk about their online interactions and reassure them that they can come forward without fear of judgment or punishment.

- **Setting Boundaries:** Establishing clear rules and boundaries for online behavior can help protect children from predators. This includes guidelines about sharing personal information, interacting with strangers online, and recognizing suspicious behavior.

Online predators represent one of the most harmful threats in the digital world, exploiting the anonymity and reach of the internet to target and manipulate children. The emotional, psychological, and long-term impacts of such exploitation can be devastating, making it crucial for parents to be vigilant and proactive in protecting their children. By understanding the tactics used by online predators and fostering open communication and trust with their children, parents can help shield them from these dangers and ensure their safety in the digital age.

4.4 Privacy Risks and Data Security

In the digital age, where information flows freely and technology affects nearly every aspect of life, privacy risks and data security have become significant concerns, especially for children. As young users navigate the internet, they often need a complete understanding of the implications of sharing personal information. This lack of awareness can make them vulnerable to a range of privacy risks and security threats that can have long-lasting consequences. For parents, understanding these risks and how they manifest is crucial to safeguarding their children's online presence.

A) The Nature of Privacy Risks and Data Security Threats

1. **What Are Privacy Risks?**

- **Personal Information Exposure:** Privacy risks primarily involve the unauthorized access, collection, or sharing of personal information. For children, this can include details such as their full name, address, phone number, date of birth, school information, and even their online habits. When exposed, this information can be exploited in various harmful ways, from identity theft to unwanted contact with strangers.
- **Behavioral Tracking:** Many websites and apps track user's behavior

online, gathering data on what they search, click on, or spend time viewing. This data is often used to build detailed profiles, which can then be sold to advertisers or, more worryingly, fall into the hands of those with malicious intent. Children, who may not fully understand the implications of behavioral tracking, can become easy targets for such practices.

1. **What Is Data Security?**

- **Data Breaches:** Data security refers to the measures taken to protect sensitive information from unauthorized access, corruption, or theft. When data is not secured correctly, it can be breached, leading to the exposure of personal information. Data breaches can occur through hacking, phishing, or other cyberattacks, and they often result in compromised information being used for fraudulent activities.
- **Inadequate Security Practices:** Children are particularly vulnerable to data security threats because they often use devices and apps that do not have vital security measures in place. Inadequate password protection, unencrypted data transmissions, and the use of unsecured Wi-Fi networks can all lead to data being intercepted or stolen.

B) The Impact of Privacy Risks on Children

1. **Identity Theft and Fraud**

- **Long-Term Consequences:** When a child's personal information is stolen, it can be used for identity theft. The thief may open credit accounts, apply for loans, or engage in other fraudulent activities in the child's name. Because children typically do not monitor their credit, these activities can go undetected for years, only coming to light when the child becomes an adult and begins using credit.
- **Financial and Legal Implications:** The financial damage caused by identity theft can be significant, impacting a child's future ability to secure loans, rent apartments, or even get a job. Additionally, sorting out the legal and financial consequences of identity theft can be a

lengthy and stressful process for both the child and their parents.

1. **Privacy Violations**

- **Unwanted Contact and Exploitation:** When children's personal information is exposed online, it can lead to unwanted contact from strangers or even online predators. This information can be used to manipulate or exploit children, putting them at significant risk. Additionally, if sensitive information such as photos or private messages is accessed, it can be shared publicly, leading to embarrassment, bullying, or worse.
- **Loss of Control over Personal Data:** Once personal information is out in the digital world, it is nearly impossible to retrieve or control. Children may lose their sense of privacy and security, knowing that their information is accessible to strangers. This loss of control can also harm trust in online platforms and lead to anxiety about future online interactions.

C) The Challenges of Ensuring Data Security

1. **Inadequate Awareness and Education**

- **Lack of Knowledge:** Many children (and even some parents) need to be fully aware of the risks associated with sharing personal information online. They may need help understanding the importance of protecting data or how easily it can be accessed and misused. This lack of knowledge can lead to careless behavior, such as using weak passwords, sharing too much information on social media, or clicking on suspicious links.
- **Complexity of Digital Security:** Ensuring data security involves understanding and implementing various security measures, such as encryption, secure passwords, and privacy settings. For many children, these concepts are complex and challenging to grasp, leading to inadequate protection of their online presence.

1. **Vulnerable Platforms and Apps**

- **Unsafe Apps and Websites:** Not all digital platforms and apps are designed with security in mind, especially those targeted at children. Some apps may not encrypt data or may collect more information than necessary, putting users at risk. Additionally, free apps are often supported by advertising, which can involve tracking user's behavior and selling their data to third parties.
- **Social Engineering Threats:** Social engineering involves manipulating individuals into divulging confidential information, often by posing as a trustworthy entity. Children, who are generally more trusting and less aware of such tactics, can be particularly exposed to social engineering attacks. This can lead to them unknowingly providing personal information or downloading malicious software.

D) The Role of Parents in Protecting Children's Privacy and Data

1. **Education and Awareness**

- **Teaching Digital Literacy:** Parents need to educate their children about the importance of privacy and data security. This includes teaching them to recognize phishing attempts, understand the risks of oversharing information, and use strong, unique passwords. Digital literacy should be a vital component of a child's education, helping them navigate the online world safely.
- **Discussing Privacy Settings:** Parents should discuss and review the privacy settings on the apps and platforms their children use. This includes making profiles private, disabling location tracking, and limiting the sharing of personal information. By actively managing these settings, parents can help reduce the risk of privacy violations.

1. **Monitoring and Setting Boundaries**

- **Active Monitoring:** Regularly monitoring a child's online activity can help parents detect potential privacy risks before they become serious issues. This can involve checking the child's social media profiles, reviewing the apps they use, and discussing any new online contacts or communications.

- **Establishing Rules:** Clear rules about what information can be shared online and with whom are essential for protecting children's privacy. Parents should establish guidelines around what constitutes personal information, the risks of sharing this information, and how to report any concerns or suspicious activities.

Privacy risks and data security are critical aspects of protecting children in the digital age. The exposure of personal information and the potential for data breaches present significant threats that can have long-lasting impacts on a child's life. By understanding these risks and taking proactive steps to educate, monitor, and protect, parents can play a crucial role in safeguarding their children's online presence. Ensuring that children are aware of the importance of privacy and data security is not just about protecting them today but also about preparing them for a future where digital literacy and security awareness will be indispensable skills.

4.5 Addiction and Overuse

As digital devices become ever more integrated into daily life, the risk of addiction and overuse has emerged as a significant concern, especially for children and teenagers. The accessibility and allure of smartphones, tablets, gaming consoles, and social media platforms make it easy for young users to spend excessive amounts of time online, often to the harm of their physical health, mental well-being, and social relationships. Understanding the nature of digital addiction and the factors that contribute to overuse is crucial for parents who want to guide their children toward healthier digital habits.

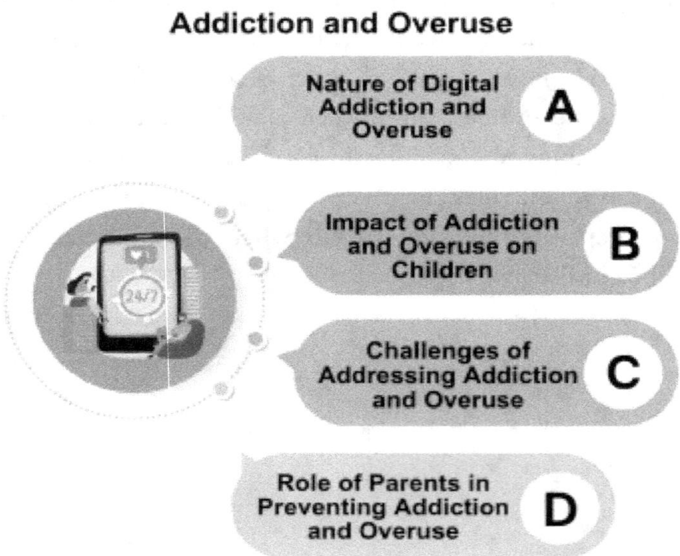

A) The Nature of Digital Addiction and Overuse

1. **What Is Digital Addiction?**

- **Definition and Characteristics**: Digital addiction refers to an obsessive need to engage with digital devices and online content, often at the expense of other essential aspects of life. This can include excessive use of social media, video games, streaming services, or even browsing the internet. Children who are addicted may find it difficult to disconnect from their devices, even when they are aware of the negative consequences.

- **Signs of Addiction:** The signs of digital addiction can be slight at first but often escalate over time. These signs may include an obsession with digital activities, irritability or anxiety when not using a device, neglecting responsibilities or hobbies in favor of screen time, and a persistent desire to return to the device even after long periods of use.

1. **How Overuse Develops**

- **Engaging Design:** Many digital platforms are designed to maximize user engagement through features like infinite scrolling, autoplay, notifications, and reward systems. These design elements can create a cycle of instant satisfaction that encourages prolonged use, making it difficult for children to stop once they start.
- **Social Pressure and FOMO:** The fear of missing out (FOMO) is a powerful motivator for digital overuse, particularly on social media platforms. Children may feel pressured to stay connected, respond to messages immediately, or keep up with the latest trends and conversations, leading to an unhealthy attachment to their devices.
- **Escapism and Coping Mechanism:** For some children, digital devices offer an escape from the challenges of the real world. Whether it is stress from school, social anxiety, or family issues, the digital world can become a coping mechanism where they can avoid their problems by immersing themselves in games, videos, or social media.

B) The Impact of Addiction and Overuse on Children

1. **Physical Health Effects**

- **Inactive Lifestyle:** Prolonged use of digital devices often leads to an inactive lifestyle, where children spend long hours sitting and staring at screens. This lack of physical activity can contribute to a range of health problems, including obesity, poor cardiovascular health, and weakened muscles and bones.

- **Sleep Disruption:** Screens emit blue light, which can interfere with the production of melatonin, a hormone that regulates sleep. Children who use digital devices late into the night may struggle to fall asleep, leading to sleep deprivation, fatigue, and a reduced ability to concentrate during the day.
- **Eye Strain and Posture Issues:** Excessive screen time can lead to digital eye strain, characterized by symptoms such as headaches, blurred vision, and dry eyes. Poor posture while using devices can also cause neck, back, and shoulder pain, potentially leading to long-term posture issues.

1. **Mental Health and Emotional Well-Being**

- **Increased Anxiety and Depression:** The pressure to stay constantly connected, coupled with exposure to harmful content and online interactions, can contribute to increased levels of anxiety and depression in children. The addictive nature of social media and gaming can exacerbate these issues, as children may feel trapped in a cycle of needing to engage with digital content to feel validated or accepted.
- **Reduced Attention Span:** The fast-paced nature of digital content, with its constant notifications and quick rewards, can affect a child's ability to focus on tasks that require maintained attention. This can impact their academic performance, as well as their ability to engage in deep, meaningful activities outside of the digital world.
- **Emotional Disturbance:** Children who are addicted to digital devices may struggle with emotional regulation, becoming irritable, angry, or upset when their screen time is limited or taken away. This emotional volatility can strain relationships with family and peers and make it difficult for children to manage stress in healthy ways.

1. **Social and Academic Consequences**

- **Isolation and Social Withdrawal:** While digital devices can facilitate social interaction, they can also lead to isolation when overused. Children who spend excessive time online may neglect face-to-face interactions, leading to a decline in real-world social skills and a sense of disconnection from family and friends.

- **Academic Decline:** The distraction of digital devices can interfere with a child's ability to focus on schoolwork, leading to a decline in academic performance. Children who prioritize screen time over studying may struggle to keep up with their assignments, miss deadlines, or perform poorly on tests and exams.
- **Decline of Hobbies and Interests:** Overuse of digital devices can decrease time for other vital activities, such as hobbies, sports, and creative pursuits. Children who become focused on digital content may lose interest in activities that once brought them joy, leading to a narrower and less fulfilling range of experiences.

C) The Challenges of Addressing Addiction and Overuse

1. Understanding the Root Causes

- **Psychological Triggers:** To effectively address digital addiction and overuse, it is essential to understand the psychological triggers that drive these behaviors. This can include factors like low self-esteem, social anxiety, or a desire for validation, all of which can be heightened by the feedback loops created by social media and gaming platforms.
- **Environmental Factors:** The environment in which a child uses digital devices can also significantly influence their level of addiction. Factors such as unsupervised access to devices, a lack of alternative activities, and the behavior modelled by parents and friends can all contribute to overuse.

1. Balancing Freedom and Control

- **Setting Boundaries:** While children need to have some freedom in their digital lives, setting clear boundaries around screen time is essential for preventing addiction. This can include establishing rules about when and where devices can be used, setting limits on the amount of time spent on specific activities, and encouraging regular breaks.

- **Consistency and Enforcement:** Enforcing screen time limits consistently is critical to preventing overuse. Parents should work together to establish and maintain these limits, ensuring that rules are applied consistently across all devices and digital activities. This may also involve setting an excellent example by exercising healthy digital habits themselves.

1. **Addressing Resistance and Setbacks**

- **Managing Resistance:** Children who are addicted to digital devices may resist attempts to limit their screen time, leading to conflicts and power struggles. Parents need to approach these situations with empathy, understanding that digital addiction is a natural and challenging issue. Working together to find mutually acceptable solutions can help reduce resistance and encourage cooperation.
- **Preventing Setbacks:** Even after successfully reducing screen time, there is always the risk of setbacks, where a child returns to old habits. Regular check-ins, ongoing communication, and a focus on building a balanced lifestyle can help prevent setbacks and ensure that children maintain healthy digital habits.

D) The Role of Parents in Preventing Addiction and Overuse

1. **Education and Awareness**

- **Teaching Healthy Habits:** Parents play a crucial role in educating their children about the importance of balance in their digital lives. This includes discussing the potential dangers of overuse, encouraging alternative activities, and promoting the benefits of a well-rounded lifestyle that includes physical exercise, social interaction, and creative pursuits.
- **Monitoring and Guidance:** Regularly monitoring a child's screen

time and guiding them toward healthier habits is essential for preventing addiction. Parents should be aware of the signs of overuse and take proactive steps to address any issues before they become serious problems.

1. **Creating a Balanced Digital Environment**

- **Encouraging Offline Activities:** One of the most effective ways to prevent digital overuse is to encourage a variety of offline activities. This can include sports, hobbies, family outings, and other forms of entertainment that do not involve screens. By providing alternative ways to have fun and relax, parents can help reduce their children's reliance on digital devices.
- **Building Strong Relationships:** Fostering strong family relationships can help reduce the likelihood of digital addiction. When children feel connected and supported at home, they are less likely to seek validation or escape in the digital world. Regular family activities, open communication, and a supportive environment contribute to a healthier balance between digital and real-life experiences.

Digital addiction and overuse are pressing concerns in today's technology-driven world, particularly for children who are still developing their habits and understanding of balance. The physical, mental, and social impacts of excessive screen time can be profound, making it essential for parents to be attentive and proactive in addressing these issues. By understanding the factors that contribute to addiction, setting clear boundaries, and fostering a balanced lifestyle, parents can help their children develop a healthier relationship with digital technology, ensuring that it enhances rather than detracts from their overall well-being.

4.6 Phishing and Online Scams

Phishing and online scams are among the most common and deceptive threats in the digital world, posing significant risks to children and teenagers who may not fully understand how these schemes operate. These malicious activities are designed to trick users into revealing sensitive information, such as passwords, credit card numbers, or personal identification details, often leading to identity theft, financial loss, and other forms of exploitation. For parents, understanding how phishing and online scams work and how to protect their children from falling victim to them is essential in today's interconnected world.

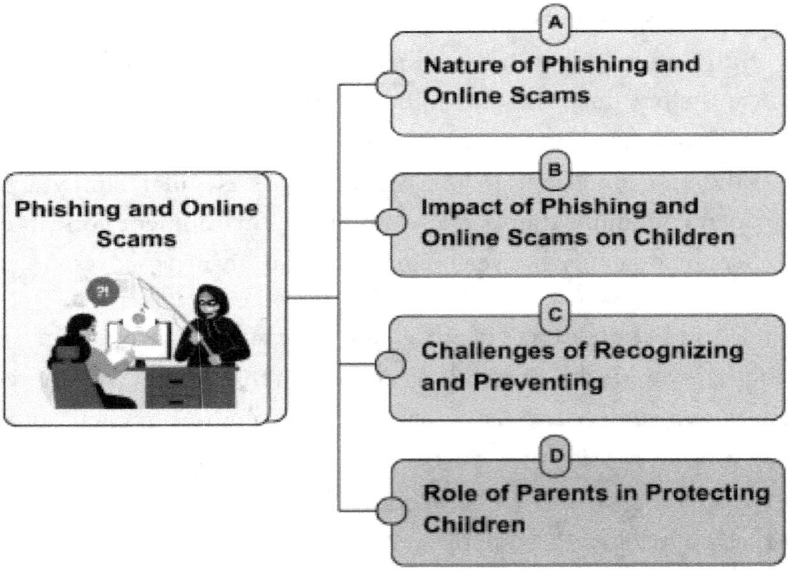

A) The Nature of Phishing and Online Scams

1. **What Is Phishing?**

- **Definition and Techniques:** Phishing is a type of cyber-attack where attackers disguise themselves as legitimate entities—such as banks, social media platforms, or online services—to deceive users into providing personal information. These attacks are typically conducted through emails, text messages, or fake websites that closely imitate the real ones. Phishing attacks often use urgent language, threats, or promises of rewards to attract victims into responding quickly without thinking critically.

- **Types of Phishing Attacks:** Phishing attacks come in various forms, each designed to deceive users into revealing sensitive information. Email phishing involves fraudulent emails that appear to be from legitimate sources, often containing links to fake websites or malicious attachments. Spear phishing is a more targeted approach aimed at specific individuals using personalized information to make the attack more convincing. Smishing occurs through SMS text messages, where links or phone numbers direct victims to fraudulent sites or automated systems that steal information. Vishing, or voice phishing, involves phone calls where attackers pose as trusted entities to extract personal details. Clone phishing involves copying a legitimate email, slightly altering it with malicious links or attachments, and then sending it to the victim. Whaling is a type of spear phishing that targets high-profile individuals with the goal of stealing sensitive information or money.

1. **What Are Online Scams?**

- **Common Online Scams:** Online scams enclose a wide range of fraudulent activities designed to deceive users for financial gain or personal information. These can include fake online shopping sites, lottery scams, "too-good-to-be-true" offers, and fraudulent job postings. Scammers often use social engineering techniques to manipulate victims into taking actions that benefit the scammer, such as transferring money or providing sensitive data.
- **Social Media and Gaming Scams:** Children and teenagers who spend significant time on social media and online gaming platforms are increasingly targeted by scams specific to these environments. These can include fake giveaways, phishing links disguised as game rewards, or scams involving virtual currency or in-game items.

B) The Impact of Phishing and Online Scams on Children

1. Financial and Identity Theft Risks

- **Unintentional Financial Loss:** Children who may not fully understand the value of money or the implications of sharing financial information can easily fall victim to phishing schemes that ask for credit card numbers or online banking details. This can lead to unauthorized purchases, drained accounts, or even long-term financial damage if their identity is stolen.
- **Identity Theft:** When a child's personal information is stolen through phishing or scams, it can be used for identity theft. This could involve opening new credit accounts, applying for loans, or committing other fraudulent activities in the child's name. Identity theft can go unnoticed for years, only becoming apparent when the child reaches adulthood and begins to use their credit.

1. Emotional and Psychological Effects

- **Fear and Anxiety:** Being targeted by a phishing attack or scam can be a frightening experience for a child. They may feel scared, guilty, or ashamed, especially if they realize they have been tricked into sharing personal information. This can lead to anxiety about using the internet and a general mistrust of online interactions.
- **Loss of Confidence:** Children who fall victim to online scams may suffer a loss of confidence in their ability to navigate the digital world safely. This can affect their willingness to engage in online activities, participate in social media, or use online resources for learning and entertainment.

C) The Challenges of Recognizing and Preventing Phishing and Online Scams

1. Deceptive Tactics

- **Realistic and Convincing Messages:** Phishing emails and scam websites are often designed to look very similar to legitimate ones, making it difficult even for adults to distinguish between the two. Children who may not have developed the critical thinking skills needed to spot these deceptions are particularly at risk.

- **Exploiting Trust and Curiosity:** Scammers often exploit the natural trust and curiosity of children by crafting messages that seem friendly, exciting, or urgent. For example, a child might receive a message claiming they have won a prize, with instructions to click a link or provide personal details to claim it. The excitement of the potential reward can easily override any suspicion.

1. **Widespread and Constant Threat**

- **Widespreadness of Attacks:** Phishing and scams are widespread across all digital platforms, from email and social media to gaming and messaging apps. The sheer volume of these attacks makes it likely that children will encounter them at some point, even if they are cautious online.
- **Evolving Tactics:** Scammers continually evolve their tactics to bypass security measures and exploit new vulnerabilities. This constant evolution means that children and parents need to stay informed about the latest threats and how to protect against them.

D) The Role of Parents in Protecting Children from Phishing and Online Scams

1. **Education and Awareness**

- **Teaching Recognition Skills:** One of the most effective ways to protect children from phishing and scams is to teach them how to recognize the warning signs. Parents should educate their children about the standard features of phishing attempts, such as unfamiliar email addresses, poor grammar, and suspicious links. Additionally, children should be taught to be careful of uninvited messages that ask for personal information or make offers that seem too good to be true.

- **Encouraging Suspicion**: A healthy level of suspicion can help children avoid falling victim to scams. Parents should teach their children to question the authenticity of unexpected messages or requests for information and verify the source before taking any action. This includes not clicking on links or downloading attachments from unknown senders.

1. **Monitoring and Setting Boundaries**

- **Supervising Online Activity:** Regular monitoring of a child's online activity can help parents spot potential phishing attempts or scams before they cause harm. This can include reviewing emails, social media interactions, and messages on gaming platforms. Parents should also encourage their children to report any suspicious messages they receive so that they can address the issue together.
- **Establishing Safe Practices:** Clear rules about online behavior are essential for protecting children from phishing and scams. These can include guidelines about not sharing personal information online, avoiding clicking on unknown links, and constantly checking with a parent before responding to any suspicious messages.

1. **Using Security Tools**

- **Anti-Phishing Software:** Many internet security programs offer anti-phishing features that can help identify and block phishing attempts. Parents should ensure that these tools are installed and kept up-to-date on all devices their children use. Additionally, enabling spam filters and pop-up blockers can reduce the chances of children encountering phishing attempts.
- **Parental Controls and Safe Browsing:** Implementing parental controls and using safe browsing tools can help minimize the risk of children accessing scam websites or falling victim to phishing attempts. These tools can restrict access to certain types of content, alert parents to suspicious activity, and provide a safer online

environment for children.

Quick tips to Avoid Phishing

1. Bookmark official websites and teach kids how to use them. This could be school logins, sports, online games or email logins.
2. Make sure to use MFA (multi-factor authentication) on all important accounts
3. Teach kids not to download apps without asking parents
4. If someone offers free games, money or products it's probably a scam
5. If you get a message "you have been hacked" or "your account will be deleted" wait and ask them to let parents know immediately.
6. Only login from the official websites and never from random links
7. Always use strong passwords on all websites
8. Never share login and password with anyone on the internet or with friends
9. Educate kids on how to spot a scam or a fraud email
10. When in doubt- never click and always ask

Phishing and online scams are ever-present threats in the digital world, posing significant risks to children who may not fully understand how these schemes work. The consequences of falling victim to such attacks can be severe, ranging from financial loss and identity theft to emotional distress and a loss of confidence in online interactions. By educating their children about the dangers of phishing and scams, monitoring their online activities, and implementing strong security measures, parents can play a crucial role in protecting their children from these deceptive and harmful practices. Ensuring that children are equipped with the knowledge and tools to navigate the digital world safely is a critical component of modern parenting, helping to build a foundation of trust and security in their online experiences.

4.7 Malware and Viruses

In the interconnected digital landscape, malware and viruses represent some of the most common and damaging threats to online security, particularly for children who may not recognize the warning signs of an infected device. These malicious software programs are designed to infiltrate, damage, or gain unauthorized access to computers, smartphones, and other devices, leading to data theft, system malfunctions, and a host of other issues. For parents, understanding how malware and viruses operate, as well as the risks they pose to their children's devices and personal information, is essential for maintaining a safe digital environment.

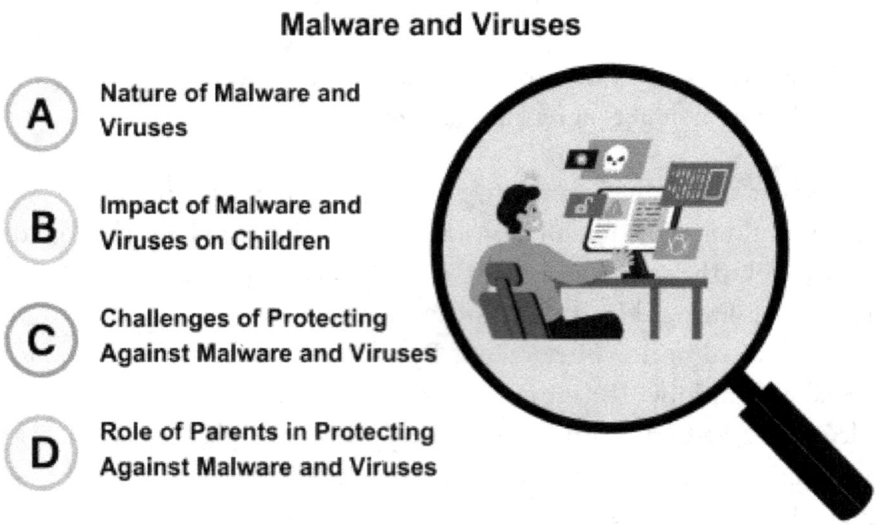

A) The Nature of Malware and Viruses

1. **What Are Malware and Viruses?**

- **Definition and Types:** Malware (short for malicious software) is a broad category of software designed to harm or exploit any programmable device, service, or network. Viruses, a specific type of malware, attach themselves to legitimate programs or files and spread throughout a device or network, replicating and causing damage. Other types of malware include worms, which spread without user interaction; ransomware, which locks users out of their devices until a ransom is paid; spyware, which secretly monitors user activity; and trojans, which disguise themselves as legitimate software to deceive users into installing them.

- **How They Spread:** Malware and viruses can spread through various means, including email attachments, malicious websites, software downloads, infected USB drives, and even social media links. Children are particularly vulnerable because they may be more likely to download free games or apps, click on unknown links, or open attachments from unfamiliar sources, all of which can introduce malware to their devices.

1. **Why Children Are Targeted**

- **Lack of Awareness:** Children often lack the experience and knowledge needed to recognize suspicious online behavior, making them prime targets for cybercriminals who use malware to gain unauthorized access to devices. They may unknowingly install malware by clicking on enticing ads, downloading unverified software, or falling for phishing schemes.
- **High-Value Targets:** While children may not have financial assets to steal, their devices can still be valuable targets for cybercriminals. Infected devices can access parent's financial information, send out spam, or be part of a large botnet—a network of infected devices used to carry out cyber-attacks. Additionally, personal information gathered from a child's device can be used for identity theft or sold on the dark web.

B) The Impact of Malware and Viruses on Children

1. **Device Damage and Data Loss**

- **System Malfunctions:** Malware and viruses can cause significant damage to a child's device, leading to slow performance, frequent crashes, and the loss of essential files. In some cases, the entire system may become unusable, requiring costly repairs or replacement. This can disrupt a child's ability to complete schoolwork, communicate with friends, or access educational resources.
- **Data Corruption and Theft:** One of the most severe consequences of malware is data theft. Malware can corrupt or delete important files, steal personal information such as photos, passwords, and documents, and even gain access to online accounts. For children, this could mean losing cherished memories, having their social media accounts hacked, or exposing sensitive family information.

1. **Privacy and Security Risks**

- **Unauthorized Access:** Malware can give cybercriminals unauthorized access to a child's device, allowing them to monitor activity, steal information, and even control the device remotely. This invasion of privacy can be particularly frightening for children, who may not understand how their information is being used or how to stop the intrusion.
- **Exposure to Inappropriate Content:** Some types of malware, such as adware, flood users with unwanted ads, including those that lead to inappropriate or harmful content. Children who are exposed to such content may experience fear, confusion, or distress, especially if the content is violent or explicit.

C) The Challenges of Protecting Against Malware and Viruses

1. **Complex and Evolving Threats**

- **Constantly Changing Landscape:** Malware and viruses are constantly evolving, with cybercriminals developing new techniques to bypass security measures and exploit vulnerabilities. This makes it challenging for even the most vigilant users to stay protected, as new threats can emerge quickly and spread widely before they are detected and neutralized.

- **Sophisticated Attack Methods:** Modern malware can be highly complicated, using advanced techniques such as polymorphism, which changes the code of the malware to avoid detection by antivirus software. This sophistication makes it difficult for traditional security measures to keep up, especially on devices used by children, who may need to update their software or security settings regularly.

1. **Inadequate Security Measures**

- **Lack of Proper Security Software:** Many children's devices do not have adequate security software installed, leaving them vulnerable to malware and viruses. Free or outdated antivirus programs may not provide sufficient protection, and children may not know how to configure or use the software they have correctly.
- **User Behavior:** Even the best security software cannot protect against all threats if the user engages in risky behavior, such as downloading files from unverified sources, clicking on suspicious links, or turning off security settings. Children, who may prioritize convenience or entertainment over safety, are particularly inclined to make these mistakes.

D) The Role of Parents in Protecting Against Malware and Viruses

1. **Education and Awareness**

- **Teaching Safe Online Practices:** One of the most effective ways to protect children from malware and viruses is to educate them about safe online practices. This includes teaching them not to click on suspicious links, download unverified files, or open email attachments from unknown sources. Children should also be taught the importance of keeping their software and apps up to date, as updates often include security patches that protect against new threats.
- **Explaining the Risks:** Parents should explain to their children how

malware and viruses work, what the consequences of an infection might be, and how they can protect themselves. By making children aware of the risks, parents can help them develop a sense of responsibility for their online safety.

1. **Implementing Strong Security Measures**

- **Installing Reliable Security Software:** Ensuring that all devices used by children have up-to-date, reliable antivirus and anti-malware software installed is crucial for protecting against threats. Parents should choose software that offers comprehensive protection, including real-time scanning, automatic updates, and the ability to detect and remove a wide range of malware.
- **Setting up Parental Controls:** Parental controls can help limit the websites and apps that children can access, reducing the likelihood of encountering malware. These controls can also prevent children from downloading unverified software or clicking on suspicious links, adding an extra layer of protection.
- **Regular Monitoring and Maintenance:** Regularly checking a child's device for signs of malware, such as slow performance, unusual pop-ups, or unexpected changes in settings, can help catch infections early. Parents should also perform routine maintenance, such as running full system scans and updating software, to ensure the device remains secure.

To summarize, here are 10 quick Tips for Kids to Stay Safe from Malware and Viruses

1. Set a rule that kids must ask their parents before downloading any apps, games, or files.
2. Turn on automatic updates on computers or phones and explain to kids why this is important.
3. Teach kids why free games or movies from unsafe websites are always risky.
4. Help them recognize urgent or flashy pop-up advertisements and

explain how these ads manipulate users into clicking.

5. Show kids why some apps or websites should not be given access to the camera or microphone.
6. If possible, use a camera cover for devices that do not have one built in.
7. Teach kids never to share their login details with anyone and to inform their parents if someone asks for them.
8. Encourage kids to speak up if their device behaves strangely or if they see unusual ads.
9. Teach kids to always ask for permission before plugging in USB drives from others.
10. Kids copy adults, so let them see you using safe websites and being cautious online.

Malware and viruses are ever-present threats in the digital world, capable of causing significant harm to both devices and personal information. Children, who may not fully understand the risks or how to protect themselves, are particularly vulnerable to these threats. By educating their children about safe online practices, installing vital security software, and actively monitoring device activity, parents can play a crucial role in safeguarding their children's digital experiences. In a world where cyber threats are constantly evolving, staying informed and proactive is essential for maintaining a secure and healthy digital environment for children. In conclusion, the digital world poses significant risks to the safety, privacy, and well-being of our children, from cyberbullying and exposure to harmful content to online predators and digital addiction. Understanding these dangers requires attention and informed guidance. The following chapters will outline specific parental measures to mitigate these risks, offering practical strategies to help parents protect their children in this complex digital landscape. By understanding and addressing these threats, parents can create a safe environment that allows their children to explore the digital world responsibly.

Chapter 5: Curating Age-Appropriate Digital Environments

As children become increasingly engaged with the digital world, parents are faced with the critical task of creating a safe and supportive online environment that aligns with their child's age and developmental needs. This chapter offers practical strategies for parents to help ensure that their children are both protected from online threats and able to explore the internet's educational and creative opportunities safely.

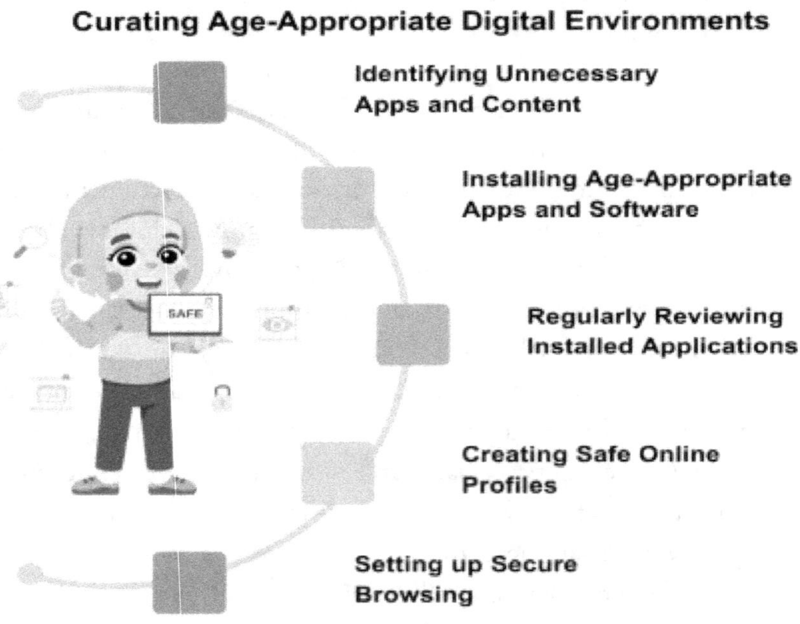

Identifying Unnecessary Apps and Content

Not all apps and content are suitable for children. Identifying and removing unnecessary or potentially harmful apps is the first step in maintaining a safe digital space for your child.

Installing Age-Appropriate Apps and Software

Choosing the right apps and software that are designed for your child's age and maturity level is crucial for promoting positive development and learning while minimizing exposure to inappropriate content.

Regularly Reviewing Installed Applications

Technology evolves quickly, and so do your child's interests and needs. Regularly reviewing and updating the apps on your child's devices ensures that their digital environment remains safe, relevant, and beneficial.

Creating Safe Online Profiles

As children start to engage more actively online, it is essential to guide them in creating secure online profiles that protect their personal information and limit exposure to online risks.

Setting up Secure Browsing

Finally, setting up secure browsing practices helps safeguard your child's online activities, protect them from harmful websites, and ensure their personal information remains private.

As we move forward in this chapter, each of these strategies will be explored in greater detail, providing you with specific guidance on how to implement them effectively. From understanding the risks associated with unnecessary apps to establishing secure browsing habits, this chapter will equip you with the tools and knowledge needed to maintain a digital environment that supports your child's growth and safety. By taking these proactive steps; parents can create a balanced and enriching online experience for their children, helping them navigate the digital world with confidence and security.

5.1 First Steps in Cybersecurity for Young Kids

Introducing young children to the digital world is a key milestone, and it is essential to start with a solid foundation in cybersecurity. As children begin exploring the internet and using digital devices, parents need to take proactive steps to ensure their safety and protect them from online threats. The initial steps in cybersecurity for young kids involve creating a safe, controlled environment that promotes positive online experiences while minimizing risks.

A) Establishing Basic Safety Rules

- **Understanding Online Safety:** Begin by explaining the internet in simple, age-appropriate terms. Help children understand that while the internet is a place to learn and have fun, it requires caution, just like the real world.
- **Setting Clear Boundaries:** Establish straightforward rules for internet use, such as not talking to strangers, not sharing personal information, and asking for permission before downloading anything.

B) Parental Involvement and Supervision

- **Active Supervision:** Always supervise young children while they use the internet. Sit with them as they explore age-appropriate websites or play online games to ensure their safety and reinforce positive behaviors.

- **Engaging Together:** Participate in your child's online activities, whether it is playing games together or watching educational videos. This builds trust and helps guide them toward making safe choices online.

C) Implementing Basic Security Measures

- **Creating Child-Friendly Profiles:** Set up separate user accounts for your children on shared devices with restricted access to ensure they can only access age-appropriate content. Use simple passwords and explain their importance.
- **Safe Browsing and Apps:** Only install apps and software designed for young children, and use kid-friendly browsers to limit access to inappropriate websites. Regularly check for updates to keep these apps secure.

D) Regular Monitoring and Updates

- **Reviewing Installed Apps:** Regularly review the apps on your child's device, removing any that are no longer needed or do not meet safety standards. This keeps their digital environment secure and age-appropriate.
- **Monitoring Online Activity:** Track your child's online activity, including the websites they visit and the people they interact with, to identify potential risks and take action if needed.
- **Teaching the Importance of Updates:** Explain to children that just like toys need maintenance, digital devices and apps need updates to stay safe and function properly.

The first steps in cybersecurity for young kids involve establishing safety rules, ensuring parental involvement, and implementing basic security measures. By creating a safe and age-appropriate digital environment, parents can guide their children's early online experiences positively, preparing them for more responsible internet use as they grow older. As we progress in this chapter, we will explore strategies such as identifying unnecessary apps, installing age-appropriate software, and setting up secure browsing. This structured approach will help parents build a comprehensive cybersecurity framework tailored to their child's developmental stage, ensuring a safe and facilitating digital environment.

5.2 Identifying Unnecessary Apps and Content

As children explore the digital world, parents need to ensure that their devices are filled with appropriate and safe content. Identifying and removing unnecessary apps and content is crucial in creating an age-appropriate digital environment. This step reduces the risk of exposure to harmful material and helps children focus on educational and constructive activities.

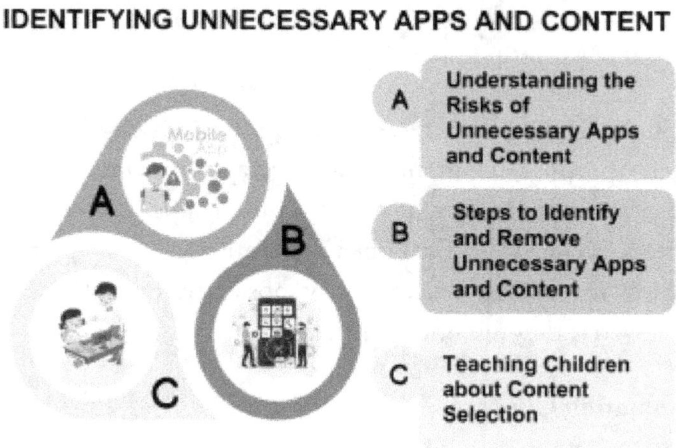

A) Understanding the Risks of Unnecessary Apps and Content

1. Potential Dangers

- Inappropriate Material: Unnecessary or unsupervised apps can expose children to unsuitable content, such as violent games or apps that allow contact with strangers. Even seemingly harmless apps might contain ads or in-app purchases leading to inappropriate content.
- Privacy and Security Risks: Many apps, even those designed for children, collect personal data. Apps with flexible privacy policies or those that collect unnecessary permissions can put your child's information at risk.

1. **Impact on Development**

- Distraction from Learning: Entertainment-focused apps can distract children from educational resources, leading to an imbalance where entertainment overshadows learning.
- Overuse and Addiction: An excess of apps can lead to excessive screen time and digital addiction. Limiting apps helps encourage a healthier balance of activities.

B) Steps to Identify and Remove Unnecessary Apps and Content

1. **Regular App Reviews**

- App Audit: Regularly review the apps on your child's device, checking their purpose, content, and age-appropriateness. Remove any outdated, unnecessary, or no longer used apps.
- Check Permissions: Examine the permissions each app requests. Apps asking for excessive access may pose privacy risks and should be removed if they are not essential.

1. **Evaluating Content**

- Use Age Ratings and Reviews: Refer to age ratings and user reviews to determine whether an app is appropriate for your child.
- Test Content Yourself: Before allowing your child to use a new app, test it yourself to ensure it is suitable and safe.

1. **Using Parental Controls**

- Implement Parental Controls: Use parental control features to restrict access to apps and content that are not age-appropriate.
- Set App Store Restrictions: Most app stores allow parents to restrict downloads based on age ratings, preventing children from downloading inappropriate apps.

C) Teaching Children about Content Selection

1. **Encouraging Thoughtful Choices**

- Guide Content Decisions: Teach your child to choose apps thoughtfully, explaining the difference between educational and entertainment-focused apps.
- Set Expectations: Involve your child in selecting apps and set clear expectations about the types of content that are acceptable.

1. **Promoting a Balanced Digital Diet**

- Limit Screen Time: Establish screen time limits and encourage a balance of educational apps, creative tools, and offline activities.
- Reinforce Positive Choices: Praise your child for choosing educational and beneficial apps, helping them build good digital habits.

By successfully identifying and removing unnecessary apps and content, you have taken a significant step in creating a safe and enriching digital environment for your child. Your efforts in regularly auditing apps, using parental controls, and guiding your child in making thoughtful choices have not gone unnoticed. This approach aligns with the goal of facilitating a secure and supportive digital environment for children, and your dedication is a testament to your commitment to your child's digital safety and education.

5.3 Installing Age-Appropriate Apps and Software

As children undertake their digital journey, parents' responsibility to ensure they have access to age-appropriate apps and software cannot be overstated. The apps and software they use can significantly impact their learning, development, and overall well-being. By carefully selecting and installing content that suits their age and maturity level, parents can positively influence their children's digital experiences.

Installing Age-Appropriate Apps and Software

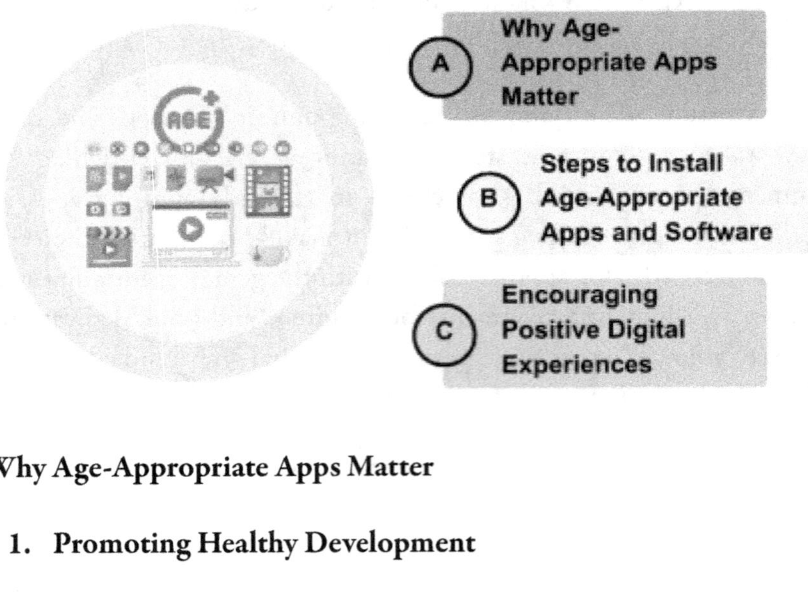

A) Why Age-Appropriate Apps Matter

1. **Promoting Healthy Development**

- **Educational Value:** Apps designed for different developmental stages help reinforce learning engagingly, catering to basic skills for younger children and critical thinking for older ones.
- **Safe Exploration:** Age-appropriate apps provide a controlled environment where children can explore and learn safely without exposure to content that may be confusing or harmful.

1. **Reducing Exposure to Risks**

- **Avoiding Inappropriate Content:** Installing only age-appropriate apps reduces the risk of children encountering unsuitable material, such as violence or complex themes.
- **Minimizing Security Risks:** Age-appropriate apps often include built-in safety features like parental controls and restrictions on in-app purchases, protecting children from security threats.

B) Steps to Install Age-Appropriate Apps and Software

1. **Research and Selection**

- **Using Trusted Sources:** Select apps from trusted sources, such as educational websites and app stores with verified age ratings, to ensure they are safe and suitable for your child.
- **Checking Age Ratings and Reviews:** Pay attention to age ratings and reviews to verify whether an app is appropriate, avoiding those with hidden risks.

1. **Testing Apps Before Installation**

- **Trying the App Yourself:** Test the app to assess its content and ensure it aligns with your child's needs and your family's values. This also allows you to set up necessary parental controls.
- **Evaluating Content and Features:** Check for in-app purchases, ads, or social features that could pose risks, ensuring the app is appropriate for your child's age.

1. **Setting up Parental Controls**

- **Configuring App Settings:** You can set up parental controls to restrict access to certain features, such as turning off in-app purchases or limiting usage time.
- **Monitoring App Usage:** Regularly monitor your child's use of the app to ensure it continues to meet their needs and is used safely.

C) Encouraging Positive Digital Experiences

1. **Balancing Educational and Entertainment Apps**

- **Encouraging a Balanced Digital Diet:** Include both educational and age-appropriate entertainment apps to provide a well-rounded digital experience that is enriching and not overly focused on entertainment.
- **Promoting Creativity and Exploration:** Choose apps that encourage creativity and critical thinking, such as those that allow children to create art or solve puzzles.

1. **Involving Children in the Selection Process**

- **Empowering Choices:** Involve your child in selecting apps from a curated list of safe options, helping them take an active role in their digital experiences.
- **Discussing App Usage:** Talk to your child about why certain apps are chosen and encourage open communication about their experiences and any questions they have.

Installing age-appropriate apps and software is a critical step in creating a safe and supportive digital environment for your child. By carefully selecting and configuring apps that align with their age and developmental needs, you ensure their digital experiences are both educational and enjoyable. As we progress in this chapter, we will explore further strategies, such as reviewing installed applications, creating safe online profiles, and setting up secure browsing to enhance your child's cybersecurity and overall well-being. This approach supports the goal of guiding children toward responsible and safe digital practices.

5.4 Regularly Reviewing Installed Applications

In today's fast-paced digital environment, new apps are constantly being developed, offering a wide range of experiences for users, including children. While many apps are educational and entertaining, parents need to review the applications installed on their children's devices regularly. This practice helps ensure that the digital environment remains safe, age-appropriate, and aligned with the family's values. Regular reviews can prevent exposure to harmful content, protect privacy, and maintain a balanced digital experience for children.

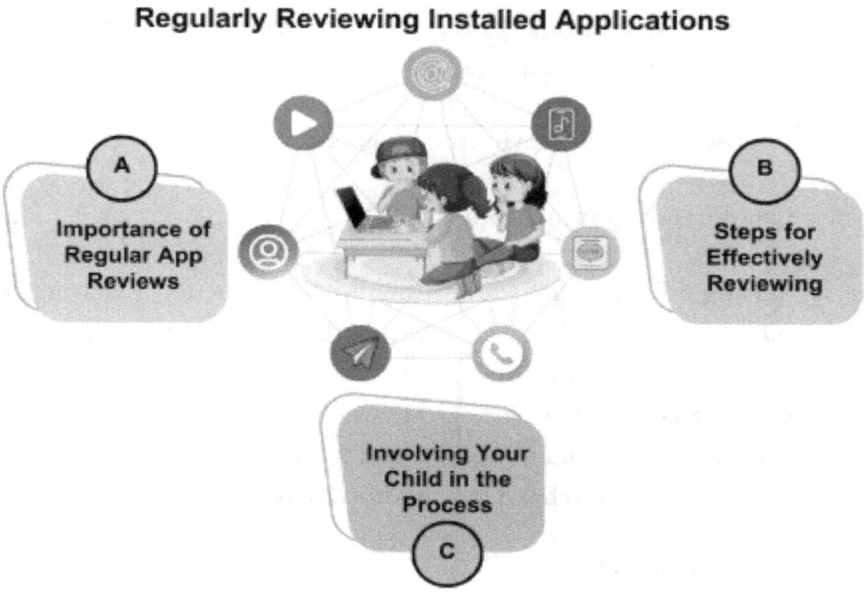

A) The Importance of Regular App Reviews

1. Maintaining a Safe Digital Environment

- **Identifying Inappropriate Content:** As children grow, they may download apps that are not suitable for their age. Regular reviews help parents remove apps with inappropriate content, such as violence or mature themes.

- **Preventing Exposure to Risks:** Some apps may have hidden dangers, like in-app purchases or social features that expose children to online strangers. Reviewing apps regularly allows parents to eliminate these risks before they cause harm.

1. **Ensuring Privacy and Security**

- **Monitoring Permissions:** Many apps request access to personal information. Regular reviews allow parents to monitor and adjust app permissions to protect their child's privacy.
- **Updating Security Measures:** Outdated apps may have security vulnerabilities. Regularly checking and updating apps ensures that the latest security patches protect your child's device.

B) Steps for Effectively Reviewing Installed Applications

1. **Conducting Routine App Audits**

- **Setting a Review Schedule:** Establish a routine for reviewing apps, such as monthly or weekly, to ensure that only relevant and safe apps remain on the device.
- **Categorizing Apps:** During the review, categorize apps into groups like educational, entertainment, and utility. This helps assess whether they serve their intended purpose and align with your child's needs.

1. **Assessing App Relevance and Usage**

- **Checking for App Usage:** Identify which apps your child uses regularly and remove those that are rarely or never used, freeing up space and reducing distractions.
- **Evaluating Educational Value:** Ensure that the apps your child uses contribute positively to their learning and development. If necessary, replace outdated apps with more age-appropriate options.

1. **Removing and Replacing Apps**

- **Deleting Unnecessary Apps:** After reviewing, delete any apps that are no longer needed, inappropriate, or pose risks to your child's safety or privacy. Explain to your child why certain apps are being removed.
- **Introducing New Apps:** Consider introducing new apps that align with your child's current interests and developmental stage, focusing on those that challenge them intellectually or spark creativity.

C) Involving Your Child in the Process

1. **Encouraging Open Communication**

- **Discussing App Usage:** Talk to your child about the apps they use and why they enjoy them. This helps you understand their interests and involve them in the decision-making process.
- **Explaining the Review Process:** Explain the importance of regularly reviewing apps to ensure they are safe and age-appropriate, empowering your child to make informed choices.

1. **Teaching Digital Responsibility**

- **Promoting Thoughtful App Selection:** Encourage your child to be selective about the apps they download, considering whether they are educational, safe, and aligned with their interests.
- **Modelling Good Digital Habits:** Lead by example by regularly reviewing and managing the apps on your own devices, demonstrating the importance of a safe and organized digital environment.

Regularly reviewing installed applications is not just a task but a crucial step in maintaining a safe, age-appropriate, and productive digital environment for children. By conducting routine app audits, assessing the relevance and safety of each app, and involving your child in the process, you are not just managing their digital experiences but also boosting your confidence in your parenting skills. This sense of accomplishment is a testament to your commitment to guiding your children toward responsible and safe digital practices.

5.5 Creating Safe Online Profiles

As children become more active online, creating safe profiles is critical to their digital experience. Whether for social media, gaming, or educational platforms, how children set up and manage their profiles significantly impacts their privacy, security, and overall safety. Guiding them in creating and maintaining safe online profiles helps protect them from potential risks while allowing them to enjoy the benefits of digital interaction.

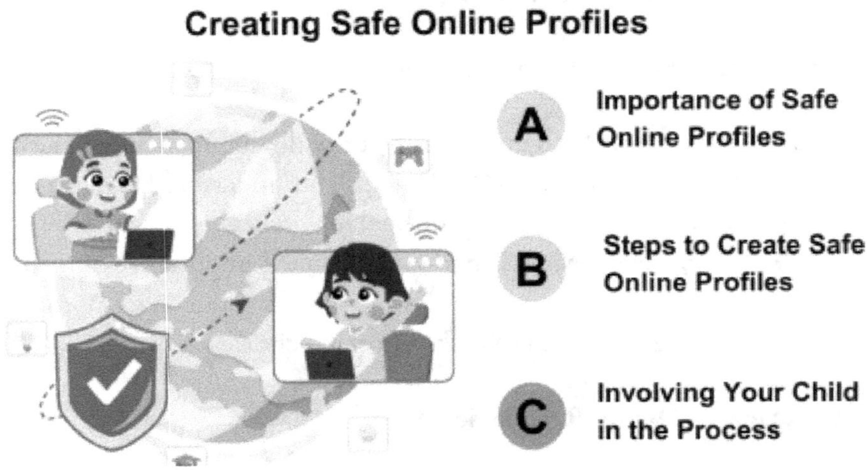

A) The Importance of Safe Online Profiles

1. Protecting Personal Information

- **Minimizing Exposure:** A safe profile limits publicly visible personal information, reducing the risk of identity theft or exploitation. Children should avoid sharing details like their full name, age, address, or school.
- **Avoiding Targeted Attacks:** Limiting shared information helps prevent targeted phishing or scams, making it harder for attackers to exploit publicly available data.

1. Maintaining Online Privacy

- **Controlling Visibility:** To protect privacy and avoid unwanted attention from strangers, set profiles to private or limit visibility to trusted contacts.
- **Managing Friend and Follower Lists:** Encourage children to accept friend requests only from people they know in real life, preventing interactions with strangers who may have malicious intentions.

B) Steps to Create Safe Online Profiles

1. **Setting up the Profile**

- **Choosing a Safe Username:** Help your child choose a username that does not reveal personal details. It should be fun and unique but not easily traceable to their real identity.
- **Using Appropriate Profile Pictures:** Choose a profile picture that does not reveal personal information. Consider using avatars or illustrations instead of personal photos.

1. **Configuring Privacy Settings**

- **Reviewing Privacy Options:** Go through privacy settings with your child, ensuring their profile is set to private and visibility is limited to approved contacts. Regularly update these settings as needed.
- **Limiting Profile Visibility:** Make sure your child's profile is not publicly searchable to prevent strangers from finding it.

1. **Managing Personal Information**

- **Being Selective about Shared Information:** Teach your child to be cautious about what they share online. Please encourage them to leave out specific details like their location or daily routine.
- **Reviewing Shared Content:** Regularly check the content your child shares to ensure it is appropriate and does not reveal too much personal information.

1. **Encouraging Safe Interactions**

- **Accepting Friend Requests Wisely:** Teach your child to be cautious when accepting friend requests, connecting only with people they know and trust.
- **Reporting and Blocking Unwanted Contacts:** Ensure your child knows how to block and report users who make them uncomfortable or engage in inappropriate behavior.

C) Involving Your Child in the Process

1. **Educating About Online Risks**

- **Discussing Privacy Importance:** Talk to your child about the risks of oversharing and the benefits of keeping certain information private.
- **Empowering Smart Choices:** Involve your child in managing their profiles, helping them make informed decisions about what to share and with whom.

1. **Modelling Safe Online Behavior**

- **Demonstrating Good Practices:** Show your child how you manage your online profiles, reinforcing the importance of privacy and safety.
- **Regular Check-ins:** Periodically review your child's online profiles together, discussing any new features or potential risks.

Creating safe online profiles is a crucial step in protecting children as they navigate the digital world. By guiding them in setting up secure profiles, managing personal information, and interacting safely online, parents can help reduce the risks associated with digital interactions. As we continue in this chapter, we will explore additional strategies, such as setting up secure browsing, to further enhance your child's cybersecurity posture and overall well-being. This approach supports the broader goal of guiding children toward responsible and safe digital practices.

5.6 Setting up Secure Browsing

As children begin to explore the internet, ensuring a secure browsing experience is crucial to protecting them from online threats. Setting up secure browsing involves using tools and practices that safeguard your child's online activities, protect their personal information, and prevent exposure to inappropriate content. By establishing a secure browsing environment, parents can help their children navigate the internet safely and responsibly.

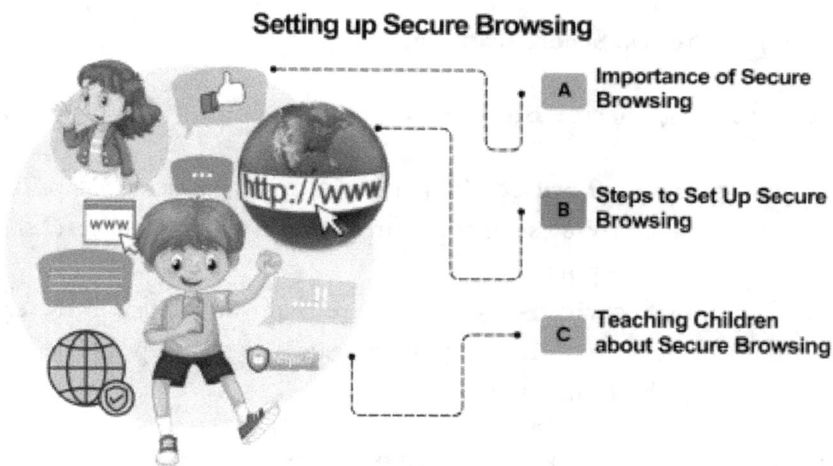

A) The Importance of Secure Browsing

1. **Protection from Online Threats**

- **Blocking Malicious Websites:** The internet is full of websites that may contain malware, phishing schemes, and other harmful content. Secure browsing tools like web filters and antivirus software help block these sites, reducing the risk of infection or data theft.
- **Preventing Unintentional Access:** Children may unintentionally come across harmful content. Secure browsing filters out inappropriate websites and search results, ensuring a safer online experience.

1. **Maintaining Privacy and Data Security**

- **Protecting Personal Information:** Secure browsing practices, such as using HTTPS connections, help protect your child's personal information from cybercriminals. Avoiding unsecured public Wi-Fi also reduces the risk of data compromise.
- **Preventing Tracking:** Many websites track user's browsing habits. Privacy-focused browsers and extensions help prevent this, keeping your child's online activities private.

B) Steps to Set Up Secure Browsing

1. **Choosing a Secure Browser**

- **Using Privacy-Focused Browsers:** Choose browsers that prioritize security and privacy, such as Firefox or Brave, which block trackers and protect against phishing.
- **Enabling Security Features:** Ensure that your child's browser has built-in security features enabled, such as pop-up blockers and warnings about suspicious websites.

1. **Implementing Web Filters and Parental Controls**

- **Setting up Web Filters:** Web filters block access to inappropriate websites and can be customized to restrict content based on categories or keywords.
- **Configuring Parental Controls:** Use parental control features to manage your child's internet access, limit browsing to approved websites, and monitor online activity.

1. **Using Secure Connections**

- **Ensuring HTTPS:** Teach your child to use websites with secure connections, such as Hypertext Transfer Protocol Secure (HTTPS), to protect their data. Look for the padlock icon in the browser's address bar to indicate a secure connection.

- **Avoiding Public Wi-Fi:** Public Wi-Fi is often unsecured and risky. Encourage your child to use a secure, private network or a Virtual Private Network (VPN) if public Wi-Fi is necessary.

1. **Regular Monitoring and Maintenance**

- **Reviewing Browser History:** Regularly check your child's browser history to ensure they are visiting safe and appropriate websites, and use this as an opportunity to discuss their online experiences.
- **Updating Browser and Security Software:** Keep your child's browser and security software up to date to maintain a secure browsing environment.

C) Teaching Children about Secure Browsing

1. **Educating About Online Risks**

- **Discussing Safe Browsing Practices:** Explain the risks of harmful content, phishing scams, and data theft. Teach your child the importance of using secure connections and being cautious about the information they share online.
- **Encouraging Responsible Behavior:** Guide your child to adopt responsible browsing habits, such as avoiding suspicious websites and not sharing personal details online.

1. **Involving Children in Security Measures**

- **Setting Rules Together:** Involve your child in setting up their secure browsing environment. Discuss the rules and explain how these measures protect them, promoting a sense of responsibility for their online safety.
- **Practicing Safe Browsing Together:** Spend time browsing the internet with your child, demonstrating safe practices and guiding them through potential risks.

Setting up secure browsing is essential for protecting children as they explore the internet. By choosing a secure browser, implementing web filters and parental controls, ensuring secure connections, and monitoring online activity, parents can create a safe browsing environment for their children. These strategies help parents feel confident that their children are better equipped to navigate the digital world safely and responsibly, aligning with the broader goal of promoting a secure and supportive digital environment for children. Curating an age-appropriate digital environment is a crucial responsibility for parents today. This chapter has provided strategies for safeguarding children's online experiences, from selecting suitable apps to creating safe online profiles and ensuring secure browsing. By implementing these measures, parents can minimize digital risks while encouraging positive and educational online interactions. In the next chapter, we will build on this foundation by exploring "Guidelines for Safe Internet Usage," offering further guidance on supporting your child's safe and responsible internet use.

Chapter 6: Guidelines for Safe Internet Usage

As children increasingly engage with the digital world, parents need to provide clear guidance on how to navigate the internet safely and responsibly. In this chapter, we will explore practical strategies that parents can implement to help their children develop healthy digital habits and stay protected from online risks. These guidelines are designed to empower both parents and children, enabling a secure and supportive environment for internet use.

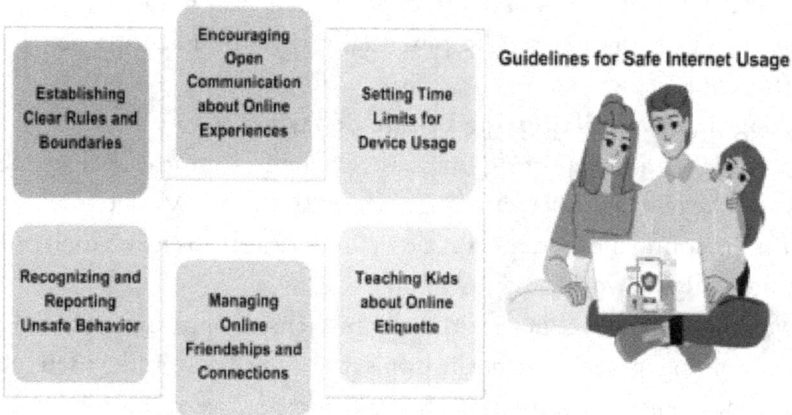

Establishing Clear Rules and Boundaries

Setting clear rules and boundaries is the foundation of safe online behavior. By defining what is acceptable and what is not, parents can help their children understand the importance of responsible internet use and the consequences of risky behaviors.

Encouraging Open Communication about Online Experiences

Open communication is crucial for maintaining a safe online environment. Encouraging your child to share their online experiences and concerns with you ensures that any potential issues are addressed early and that your child feels supported and understood.

Setting Time Limits for Device Usage

Limiting screen time is vital to maintaining a healthy balance between online and offline activities. Setting time limits helps prevent digital overuse and encourages children to engage in a variety of activities that contribute to their overall well-being.

Teaching Kids about Online Etiquette

Teaching proper online etiquette, or "netiquette," is essential for promoting respectful and positive digital interactions. By understanding the importance of appropriate behavior online, children can build healthy relationships and avoid conflicts in the digital space.

Managing Online Friendships and Connections

As children form online friendships, it is essential to guide them in managing these relationships safely. Teaching them how to identify trustworthy connections and how to handle potentially risky interactions helps protect them from online dangers

Recognizing and Reporting Unsafe Behavior

Recognizing and reporting unsafe behavior is a critical skill for children navigating the internet. By equipping them with the knowledge to identify red flags and the confidence to report issues, parents can help ensure their children's safety in the digital world.

Together, these strategies form a comprehensive approach to safe internet usage, providing parents with the tools they need to guide their children through the complexities of the online world. As we discuss each of these topics, you will gain practical insights on how to create a secure and responsible digital environment for your child.

6.1 Establishing Clear Rules and Boundaries

As children explore the digital world, parents need to establish clear rules and boundaries that guide their online behavior. These guidelines help children understand the importance of safe internet usage while providing them with the structure they need to make responsible decisions. Establishing rules and boundaries is a proactive way to prevent potential risks and ensure that your child's online experiences are positive and safe.

A) Why Clear Rules and Boundaries Are Important

1. **Promoting Safe Behavior**

- **Understanding Expectations:** Clear rules help children understand what is expected of them when they are online, reducing the likelihood of engaging in risky behaviors such as sharing personal information or interacting with strangers.
- **Consistent Guidance:** Boundaries provide a consistent framework that children can rely on as they explore the internet, helping them make safer choices even when they are not directly supervised.

1. **Preventing Online Risks**

- **Limiting Exposure to Threats:** By setting boundaries on what sites can be visited and what information can be shared, parents can minimize the chances of children encountering online threats like cyberbullying, predators, or inappropriate content.

- **Encouraging Positive Habits:** Establishing time limits and content restrictions helps prevent overuse and encourages children to develop healthy digital habits.

B) Steps to Establish Clear Rules and Boundaries

1. **Set Specific Guidelines**

- **Define Acceptable Activities:** Clearly outline which activities are allowed, such as educational games, research for school, or safe social interactions, and which are not, like visiting unapproved websites or downloading unknown apps.
- **Create Time Limits:** Establish rules around how much time your child can spend online each day. This helps prevent digital overuse and ensures that online activities are balanced with offline activities like homework, physical exercise, and family time.

1. **Communicate Expectations Clearly**

- **Discuss the Rules Together:** Involve your child in setting these rules. Explain why each rule is important, and encourage them to ask questions or express their concerns. This will help them feel more invested in following the guidelines.
- **Post the Rules Visibly:** Consider posting the rules in a visible location near the family computer or device area. This serves as a regular reminder of the agreed-upon boundaries.

1. **Enforce the Rules Consistently**

- **Monitor Compliance:** Regularly check to ensure that your child is adhering to the established rules. Consistent enforcement supports the importance of the boundaries you have set.
- **Address Violations Promptly:** If a rule is broken, address it calmly

but firmly, discussing the importance of the boundary and the consequences of not following it.

- Adapt Rules as Needed:
- **Please review and Adjust:** As your child grows and gains more online experience, review the rules and adjust them as necessary to match their developmental stage and the evolving digital landscape.
- **Encourage Ongoing Dialogue:** Keep the conversation about online safety ongoing. Encourage your child to share their online experiences and express any concerns or questions they may have.

Establishing clear rules and boundaries is a fundamental step in guiding children toward safe and responsible internet usage. By setting specific guidelines, communicating expectations, and consistently enforcing these rules, parents can create a secure online environment that supports their child's growth and well-being.

6.2 Encouraging Open Communication about Online Experiences

Open communication between parents and children is not just a tool but a key to promoting a safe and supportive online environment. By encouraging your child to talk openly about their online experiences, you can help them explore the digital world with confidence and address any challenges or concerns they may encounter. This open dialogue not only builds trust but also empowers children to make safer and more informed decisions online.

A) Why Open Communication Is Important

1. **Building Trust and Understanding**

- **Creating a Safe Space:** When children feel comfortable sharing their online experiences without fear of judgment or punishment, they are more likely to come to you with concerns or questions. This open line of communication helps you stay informed about their online activities and any potential issues they may face.
- **Strengthening Relationships:** Regular conversations about online experiences strengthen the parent-child relationship, enabling a sense of trust that is essential for guiding your child through the

complexities of the digital world.

1. **Addressing Online Risks Promptly**

- **Identifying Issues Early:** Encouraging open communication allows you to identify and address potential online risks, such as cyberbullying, exposure to inappropriate content, or interactions with strangers, before they escalate.
- **Providing Guidance and Support:** When your child shares their online experiences with you, it provides an opportunity to offer guidance, correct misconceptions, and reinforce safe online behaviors.

B) How to Encourage Open Communication

1. **Create a Non-Judgmental Environment**

- **Listen Without Interrupting:** When your child talks about their online activities, listen attentively without interrupting or immediately passing judgment. This encourages them to be more open and honest about their experiences.
- **Validate Their Feelings:** Acknowledge your child's feelings and experiences, even if they seem unimportant. Validating their emotions shows that you take their concerns seriously and are there to support them.

1. **Ask Open-Ended Questions**

- **Start Conversations Naturally:** Instead of interrogating your child about their online activities, start with open-ended questions that invite discussion. For example, ask, "What did you find interesting online today?" or "Have you seen anything online that made you uncomfortable?"
- **Encourage Sharing:** Let your child know that they can come to you with any questions or concerns about what they encounter online, no matter how small or unimportant they may seem.

1. **Share Your Own Experiences**

- **Lead by Example:** Share your own online experiences, both positive and negative, to show that exploring the digital world is something everyone deals with. This can make your child feel less isolated and more willing to share their own experiences.
- **Discuss Digital Challenges Together:** Use your own experiences as a starting point to discuss broader digital challenges, such as privacy concerns or the importance of verifying information online.

1. **Regular Check-Ins**

- **Set Aside Time for Discussions:** Make it a routine to check in with your child about their online activities. Regularly scheduled conversations help normalize discussions about the internet and ensure that communication remains open.
- **Stay Updated on Their Interests:** As your child's online interests evolve, stay engaged by learning about the platforms, games, or social media sites they use. This knowledge allows you to have more meaningful and relevant conversations with them.

1. **Be Supportive, Not Punitive**

- **Focus on Learning:** If your child encounters a problem online, focus on what can be learned from the situation rather than solely on punishment. This approach encourages them to be honest about their mistakes and helps them grow from the experience.
- **Provide Reassurance:** Reassure your child that they can come to you with any online issue and that you will work together to find a solution. This support is crucial for maintaining open communication and building their confidence in handling online challenges.

Encouraging open communication about online experiences is not just a strategy but a necessity for guiding children safely through the digital world. By creating a non-judgmental environment, asking open-ended questions, sharing your own experiences, and regularly checking in with your child, you can build a trusting relationship that promotes safe and responsible internet use.

6.3 Setting Time Limits for Device Usage

In an age where digital devices are an integral part of daily life, setting time limits for device usage is crucial for maintaining a healthy balance between online and offline activities. Excessive screen time can lead to various issues, including physical health problems, reduced academic performance, and increased exposure to online risks. By establishing clear and reasonable time limits, parents can help their children develop healthy digital habits that promote overall well-being.

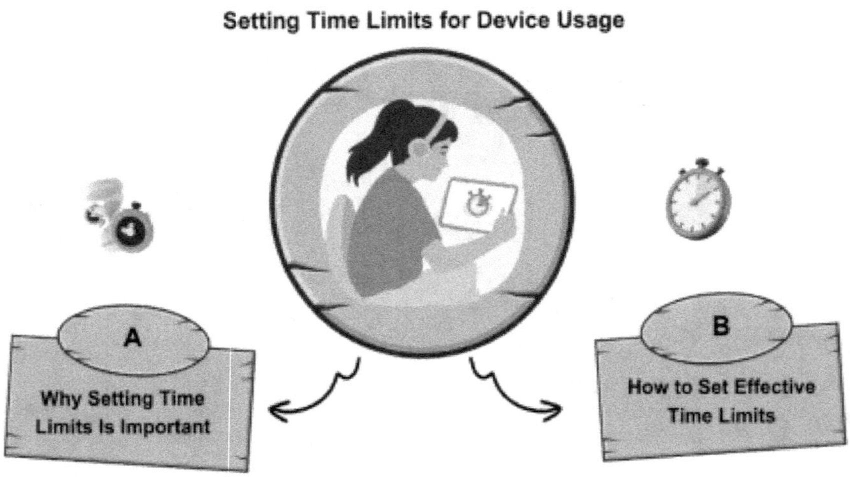

A) Why Setting Time Limits Is Important

1. **Promoting a Balanced Lifestyle**

- **Encouraging Offline Activities:** Time limits on device usage ensure that children have ample time for offline activities such as physical exercise, reading, and family interactions. This balance is essential for their physical, mental, and emotional development.
- **Reducing Digital Dependency:** Setting boundaries around screen time helps prevent children from becoming overly dependent on digital devices for entertainment and social interaction, encouraging

them to explore other hobbies and interests.

1. **Preventing Health Issues**

- **Avoiding Eye Strain and Fatigue:** Prolonged screen time can cause eye strain, headaches, and fatigue. Time limits help mitigate these physical effects by encouraging regular breaks and reducing overall screen exposure.
- **Improving Sleep Quality:** Excessive device use, especially before bedtime, can interfere with sleep patterns due to the blue light emitted by screens. Limiting device usage in the evening helps improve sleep quality and overall health.

1. **Enhancing Focus and Productivity**

- **Boosting Academic Performance:** Limiting screen time ensures that children have enough time to focus on their studies and complete their homework without the distractions of digital devices.
- **Encouraging Mindful Use:** Time limits encourage children to use their devices more mindfully, prioritizing educational and productive activities over mindless scrolling or gaming.

B) How to Set Effective Time Limits

1. **Determine Appropriate Limits**

- **Consider Age and Needs:** Define time limits to your child's age and individual needs. Younger children may require stricter limits, while older children and teenagers might need more flexibility to accommodate academic responsibilities and social interactions.
- **Use Expert Guidelines:** Refer to expert recommendations, such as those from pediatricians or child development specialists, to determine appropriate screen time for different age groups.

1. **Establish Clear Rules**

- **Set Specific Time Frames:** Define when and how long devices can be used each day. For example, you might allow one hour of screen time after homework is completed or limit device usage to certain hours of the day.
- **Create Tech-Free Zones:** Designate areas of the home, such as the dining room or bedrooms, as tech-free zones to encourage device-free family time and better sleep hygiene.

1. **Involve Your Child in the Process**

- **Discuss the Reasons for Limits:** Explain to your child why time limits are necessary, focusing on the benefits for their health, well-being, and development. Involving them in the discussion helps them understand the importance of these boundaries.
- **Agree on Consequences:** Work together to establish consequences for exceeding screen time limits. Consistent enforcement of these consequences reinforces the importance of adhering to the rules.

1. **Use Tools and Technology**

- **Set up Parental Controls:** Many devices and apps offer parental control features that allow you to set daily screen time limits, block certain apps after a set time, and monitor overall usage.
- **Use Timers and Alerts:** Implement timers or alerts that remind your child when their screen time is about to end. This helps them manage their time better and reduces the likelihood of arguments when it is time to log off.

1. **Model Good Behavior**

- **Lead by Example:** Show your child that you also adhere to time limits on device usage. Modelling balanced digital habits encourages them to follow suit and reinforces the rules you have set.
- **Engage in Offline Activities Together:** Spend time with your child doing offline activities, such as playing sports, reading, or going for

a walk. This not only limits screen time but also strengthens your relationship and promotes a healthier lifestyle.

Setting time limits for device usage is an essential part of promoting healthy digital habits in children. By establishing clear boundaries, involving your child in the process, and using tools to monitor and enforce limits, you can help ensure that their digital experiences are balanced and beneficial. As we continue in this chapter, we will explore additional strategies for safe internet usage, further enhancing your child's ability to explore the digital world responsibly.

6.4 Teaching Kids about Online Etiquette

As children become more active in the digital world, understanding and practicing proper online etiquette is crucial for their safety and social development. Online etiquette, often referred to as "netiquette," encloses the guidelines and behaviors that help maintain a respectful, safe, and positive environment in digital interactions. Teaching kids about online etiquette not only protects them from potential misunderstandings and conflicts but also enables healthy online relationships and responsible digital citizenship.

A) Why Online Etiquette Is Important

1. Promoting Respectful Interactions

- **Maintaining Civility Online:** Teaching children to communicate respectfully online helps prevent conflicts, misunderstandings, and cyberbullying. When kids understand the importance of treating others with kindness and respect, they contribute to a more positive digital environment.
- **Building Healthy Relationships:** Proper online etiquette is essential for building and maintaining healthy relationships, whether with friends, classmates, or even strangers. Respectful communication facilitates trust and understanding, which are critical components of any relationship.

1. **Protecting Personal Reputation**

- **Avoiding Negative Consequences:** In the digital age, online actions can have lasting effects on a child's reputation. Teaching kids to think before they post or share information helps them avoid behaviors that could harm their reputation or future opportunities.
- **Understanding Public:** Children need to understand that what they post online can be seen by others and may remain accessible indefinitely. Practicing good online etiquette helps them make decisions that they will not regret later.

1. **Encouraging Responsible Digital Citizenship**

- **Encouraging Accountability:** Good online etiquette involves taking responsibility for one's actions in the digital space. This sense of accountability is a fundamental aspect of being a responsible digital citizen, helping children contribute positively to online communities.
- **Learning from Mistakes:** When kids understand and practice online etiquette, they're better equipped to learn from their mistakes and correct their behavior, which is an integral part of growing up in a digital world.

B) Critical Aspects of Online Etiquette to Teach

1. **Respectful Communication**

- **Think Before You Post:** Teach children to pause and think before posting or sending a message. Encourage them to consider how others might perceive their words and whether they would say the same thing face-to-face.
- **Use Appropriate Language:** Children should learn to use polite and appropriate language in all online interactions. This includes avoiding offensive, hurtful, or aggressive language, as well as understanding the tone and context of their words.

1. **Privacy and Boundaries**

- **Respect Other's Privacy:** Emphasize the importance of respecting the privacy of others online. This means not sharing someone else's personal information, photos, or messages without their permission.
- **Understand Digital Boundaries:** Teach kids to recognize and respect the digital boundaries of others, such as knowing when it is appropriate to message someone or when to take a break from online interactions.

1. **Responsible Sharing**

- **Avoid Spreading Rumors or Misinformation:** Children should be taught not to share information that they are not sure is true. Spreading rumors or misinformation can lead to unnecessary conflict and harm.
- **Consider the Impact of Sharing:** Before sharing a post, picture, or video, encourage children to think about how it might affect others. Remind them that once something is shared online, it can be difficult to control who sees it or how it is used.

1. **Handling Disagreements Online**

- **Disagree Respectfully:** Teach children that it is okay to disagree with someone online, but it is essential to do so respectfully. Please encourage them to express their opinions calmly and avoid escalating arguments.
- **Know When to Step Away:** Sometimes, the best way to handle a disagreement is to step away from the conversation. Teach kids to recognize when it is time to log off and cool down before responding.

1. **Dealing with Cyberbullying**

- **Recognize Cyberbullying:** Help children understand what cyberbullying looks like and why it is harmful. Please encourage them to report any bullying behavior they encounter, whether they're a victim or a bystander.

- **Responding Appropriately:** Teach children how to respond to cyberbullying, including not retaliating, blocking the bully, and seeking help from a trusted adult.
- How to Reinforce Online Etiquette

1. **Lead by Example**

- **Model Good Behavior:** Children learn a lot by watching the adults around them. In your digital interactions, demonstrate good online etiquette, showing respect, responsibility, and kindness.
- **Share Your Experiences:** Discuss your own online experiences with your child, including how you handle conflicts or practice good etiquette. This helps them understand the importance of these behaviors.

1. **Create a Family Code of Conduct**

- **Set Clear Expectations:** Establish a family code of conduct for online behavior that everyone agrees to follow. This can include rules about respectful communication, privacy, and responsible sharing.
- **Please review and Update Regularly:** As your child grows and their online activities change, revisit and update your family's code of conduct to ensure it remains relevant and practical.

1. **Encourage Open Discussions**

- **Talk about Online Experiences:** Regularly discuss your child's online experiences and any challenges they face. Use these conversations as opportunities to reinforce the importance of online etiquette.
- **Provide Positive Reinforcement:** When you notice your child practicing good online etiquette, acknowledge and praise their behavior. Positive reinforcement helps build good habits and encourages continued responsible behavior.

Teaching kids about online etiquette is a vital part of preparing them for safe and responsible internet use. By promoting respectful communication, protecting personal reputation, and encouraging responsible digital citizenship, parents can help their children explore the digital world with confidence and integrity.

6.5 Managing Online Friendships and Connections

As children and teenagers increasingly engage with social media, gaming, and other online platforms, managing their online friendships and connections becomes an essential aspect of safe internet usage. Online interactions can offer valuable social opportunities, but they also pose risks if not guided carefully. Teaching kids how to manage their online friendships and connections not only helps them build positive relationships but also empowers them to protect themselves from potential dangers, establishing confidence in parents about their guidance.

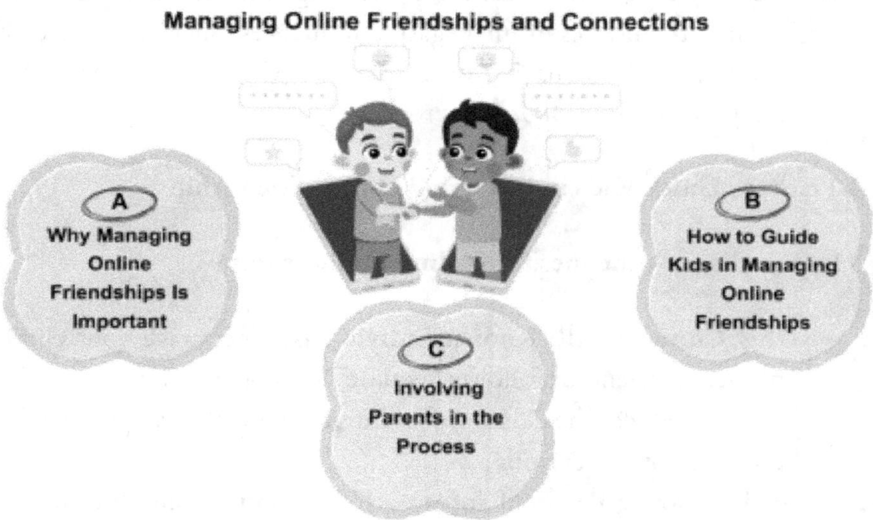

A) Why Managing Online Friendships Is Important

1. **Protecting Personal Safety**

- **Recognizing Safe Connections:** Children need to understand the difference between safe and unsafe online connections. Teaching them to be cautious about who they interact with online helps protect them from potential threats, such as online predators or cyberbullies.

- **Limiting Exposure to Risks:** By managing their online connections carefully, children can limit their exposure to risky situations, such as being pressured into sharing personal information or engaging in harmful behaviors.

1. **Promoting Positive Interactions**

- **Building Healthy Relationships:** Managing online friendships allows children to focus on positive, supportive relationships that contribute to their well-being. Encouraging them to connect with people who share their interests and values enables a healthier online experience.
- **Avoiding Negative Influences:** Teaching children to recognize and distance themselves from negative influences, such as people who encourage risky behavior or engage in cyberbullying, helps them maintain a positive digital environment.

B) How to Guide Kids in Managing Online Friendships

1. **Set Clear Guidelines for Online Connections**

- **Only Connect with Known Individuals:** Encourage your child to only accept friend or follower requests from people they know in real life. This reduces the likelihood of interacting with strangers who may have malicious intentions.
- **Avoid Sharing Personal Information:** Remind your child never to share personal information, such as their address, phone number, or school details, with online friends, even if they seem trustworthy.

1. **Teach Kids to Be Cautious with New Connections**

- **Verify New Contacts:** Before accepting a friend request from someone they do not know well, teach your child to verify the person's identity. They can do this by asking how they know them or checking with mutual friends.
- **Be Suspicious of Unwelcomed Messages:** Warn your child about

the dangers of responding to uninvited messages or friend requests, especially those that seem too good to be true or make them uncomfortable.

1. **Encourage Regular Review of Friend Lists**

- **Keep Friend Lists Updated:** Periodically review online friend lists with your child to remove any contacts they no longer interact with or those who may pose a risk. This practice helps maintain a safer and more relevant network of connections.
- **Monitor Online Interactions:** Encourage your child to pay attention to how their online friends interact with them. If someone starts acting suspiciously or makes them feel uneasy, they should be empowered to unfriend, block, or report the individual.

1. **Address Cyberbullying and Negative Interactions**

- **Recognize Signs of Cyberbullying:** Teach your child to recognize the signs of cyberbullying, such as repeated negative comments, exclusion from online groups, or pressure to engage in harmful activities. Encourage them to speak up if they experience or witness cyberbullying.
- **Know When to Disconnect:** Children need to know when to disconnect from an online friendship that has become toxic or harmful. Reassure them that it is okay to block or unfriend someone if the relationship is negatively affecting their well-being.

1. **Promote Positive Online Behaviors**

- **Be a Good Digital Friend:** Encourage your child to be a positive influence in their online communities. This includes being supportive, avoiding gossip or negative comments, and standing up for others who may be targeted by bullying or exclusion.
- **Support Safe Online Communities:** Help your child find and join online communities that are safe, supportive, and aligned with their

interests. These spaces can provide a positive outlet for social interaction and personal growth.

C) Involving Parents in the Process

1. **Maintain Open Communication**

- **Discuss Online Friendships Regularly:** Make it a habit to talk with your child about their online friendships and connections. Ask about the people they interact with, how they feel about these relationships, and if they have encountered any issues.
- **Offer Guidance Without Intruding:** While it is essential to monitor your child's online activities, strive to offer guidance without being overly intrusive. This balance helps maintain trust and encourages your child to come to you with concerns.

1. **Model Positive Online Relationships**

- **Demonstrate Healthy Online Interactions:** Show your child how to manage online relationships by modelling positive behaviors in your digital interactions. Demonstrating respect, kindness, and caution in your online friendships sets an excellent example for your child to follow.
- **Share Personal Experiences:** Share your own experiences with online friendships, both positive and negative. Discussing how you've managed these relationships can provide valuable lessons for your child.

Managing online friendships and connections is a critical skill for children as they explore the digital world. By setting clear guidelines, teaching caution with new connections, encouraging regular review of friend lists, and promoting positive online behaviors, parents can help their children build safe and supportive online relationships. This successful guidance can make parents feel proud of their parenting, knowing they have equipped their children to interact positively and responsibly in the online space.

6.6 Recognizing and Reporting Unsafe Behavior

In the digital age, children are increasingly exposed to a wide range of online interactions, some of which may pose risks to their safety and well-being. Teaching kids to recognize and report unsafe behavior is a critical component of ensuring their security in the online world. By equipping them with the knowledge and tools to identify potential dangers and take appropriate action, parents can help protect their children from harm and empower them to be responsible digital citizens.

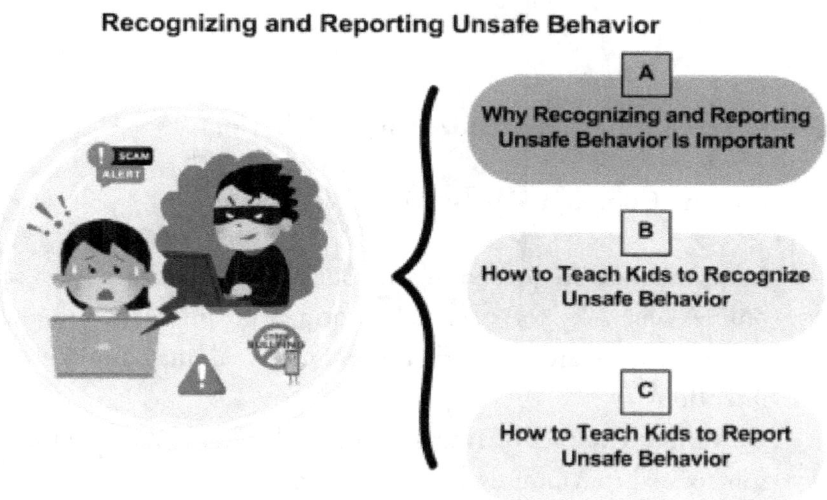

A) Why Recognizing and Reporting Unsafe Behavior Is Important

1. Protecting Children from Online Threats

- **Preventing Exploitation:** Children who can recognize unsafe behavior, such as inappropriate messages or requests for personal information, are better equipped to avoid situations that could lead to exploitation or abuse.
- **Mitigating Cyberbullying:** Awareness of cyberbullying signs enables children to identify when they or others are being targeted. Immediate

reporting can prevent further harm and initiate the necessary support measures.

1. **Empowering Children to Take Action**

- **Building Confidence in Reporting:** When children understand that they have the right and ability to report unsafe behavior, they are more likely to take action when they encounter it. This empowerment is crucial for maintaining their safety and well-being.
- **Encouraging Responsibility:** Teaching children to report unsafe behavior enables them to feel responsible for their own and other's safety, contributing to a safer online community.

B) How to Teach Kids to Recognize Unsafe Behavior

1. **Identify Common Signs of Unsafe Behavior**

- **Inappropriate Requests:** Teach your child to be cautious of anyone online who asks for personal information, photos or to meet in person. These are signs that the individual may not have good intentions.
- **Unwanted Contact or Harassment:** Help your child recognize when someone's behavior crosses the line into harassment, such as repeated unwanted messages, threats, or attempts to pressure them into uncomfortable situations.
- **Strange or Suspicious Behavior:** Encourage your child to trust their instincts. If someone online is acting in a way that feels strange, pushy, or overly familiar, it is essential to recognize this as potentially unsafe.

1. **Discuss Cyberbullying**

- **Understand What Cyberbullying Looks Like:** Explain the different forms cyberbullying can take, including hurtful comments, spreading rumors, or exclusion from online groups. Help your child understand that cyberbullying is not just a normal part of being online but a serious issue that needs to be addressed.

- **Emphasize the Importance of Reporting:** Make it clear that cyberbullying should always be reported, whether your child is the target or a witness. Reporting can stop the behavior and prevent it from escalating.

1. **Recognize Phishing and Scams**

- **Identify Suspicious Links and Messages:** Teach your child to be cautious of unexpected links, emails, or messages that ask for personal information or make offers that seem too good to be true. Phishing scams often disguise themselves as legitimate requests to trick users into revealing sensitive information.
- **Avoid Clicking on Unknown Links:** Reinforce the importance of not clicking on links from unknown or untrusted sources. This simple habit can prevent a host of security issues, from malware to data breaches.

C) How to Teach Kids to Report Unsafe Behavior

1. **Explain How to Report**

- **Use Platform Reporting Tools:** Show your child how to use the reporting tools available on social media platforms, games, and other online services. These tools are designed to help users report unsafe behavior, harassment, or inappropriate content.
- **Know When to Involve an Adult:** Make sure your child knows that they can always come to you or another trusted adult if they encounter something unsafe online. Reassure them that they will be safe for reporting an issue, and emphasize the importance of seeking help.

1. **Encourage Immediate Action**

- **Do not wait to Report:** Teach your child to report unsafe behavior as soon as they encounter it. Delaying can escalate the situation or put others at risk.
- **Document the Behavior:** Encourage your child to take screenshots or save messages that can be used as evidence when reporting. This documentation can help authorities or platform moderators take appropriate action.

1. **Reinforce the Importance of Reporting**

- **Make It a Family Rule:** Establish a family rule that any unsafe behavior encountered online must be reported immediately. This sets a clear expectation and underscores the seriousness of the issue.
- **Praise Reporting Efforts:** When your child reports unsafe behavior, acknowledge and praise their actions. Positive reinforcement helps them feel confident in their ability to recognize and respond to online threats.

1. **Provide Ongoing Support**

- **Follow Up on Reports:** After your child has reported unsafe behavior, follow up with them to ensure they are feeling okay and discuss any outcomes or further steps. This ongoing support is essential for their emotional well-being.
- **Keep the Conversation Open:** Continue to discuss online safety regularly, encouraging your child to share any concerns or experiences. Keeping the lines of communication open helps reinforce the importance of recognizing and reporting unsafe behavior.

Recognizing and reporting unsafe behavior is a critical skill for children navigating the online world. By teaching them to identify red flags, understand the importance of reporting, and take immediate action when necessary, parents can help protect their children from online threats and foster a safer digital environment. As we conclude this chapter, your child will be better equipped to manage their online interactions responsibly, ensuring their safety and well-being as they continue to explore the digital world. Establishing clear guidelines for safe internet usage, encouraging open communication, setting time limits, teaching online etiquette, managing online friendships, and recognizing and reporting unsafe behavior are all essential steps in safeguarding your child's online experiences. By implementing these strategies, you can help your child navigate the digital world with confidence and responsibility. In the next chapter, we will discuss the role of parental controls and how they can play a significant part in creating a safe and secure internet environment for your child.

Chapter 7: Implementing Parental Controls

As children increasingly explore the digital world, ensuring their safety is a top priority for parents. Parental controls are powerful tools that help manage your child's online activities, set boundaries, and protect them from potential risks. This chapter will guide you through the critical aspects of implementing parental controls, providing the knowledge you need to create a safe digital environment for your child.

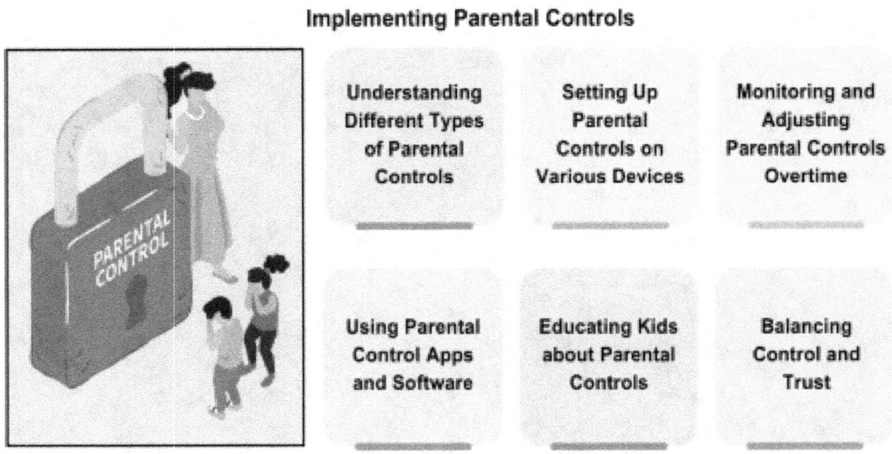

Understanding Different Types of Parental Controls

The first step in protecting your child online is understanding the various types of parental controls available. From content filters to time limits, these tools can be tailored to suit your child's age and online habits. We will explore how each type can be used effectively to ensure your child's safety.

Setting Up Parental Controls on Various Devices

Children access the internet through multiple devices, such as smartphones, tablets, and gaming consoles. Setting up parental controls on all of these devices is crucial for comprehensive protection. This section will provide practical guidance on configuring controls across different platforms.

Monitoring and Adjusting Parental Controls Overtime

As your child grows, their online behavior will change. Regularly monitoring and adjusting parental controls ensures that they continue to be effective. We will discuss the importance of ongoing oversight and how to adapt controls to your child's development.

Using Parental Control Apps and Software

Parental control apps and software are essential for managing your child's digital life. With features like content filtering and screen time management, these tools help maintain a safe online environment. This section will review some of the best options and how to use them effectively.

Educating Kids about Parental Controls

Educating your child about the reasons behind parental controls helps build trust and cooperation. In this section, we will explore how to explain these measures to your child, making them feel involved and respected.

Balancing Control and Trust

Balancing control with trust is a crucial challenge in digital parenting. While controls are necessary, they should also respect your child's need for independence. We will offer strategies for maintaining this balance, ensuring your child feels both protected and supported.

This chapter provides a concise guide to implementing parental controls, helping you create a safe and positive online experience for your child. These steps will set the foundation for responsible digital behavior as your child explores the online world.

7.1 Understanding Different Types of Parental Controls

Tools for parental supervision are essential in managing and monitoring the digital footprints of young users, ensuring a secure browsing experience. With a variety of content available online, it becomes crucial to discuss the different parental tools available and use them to shield young minds from potential online threats. This section provides insights into various parental controls and their specific utilities.

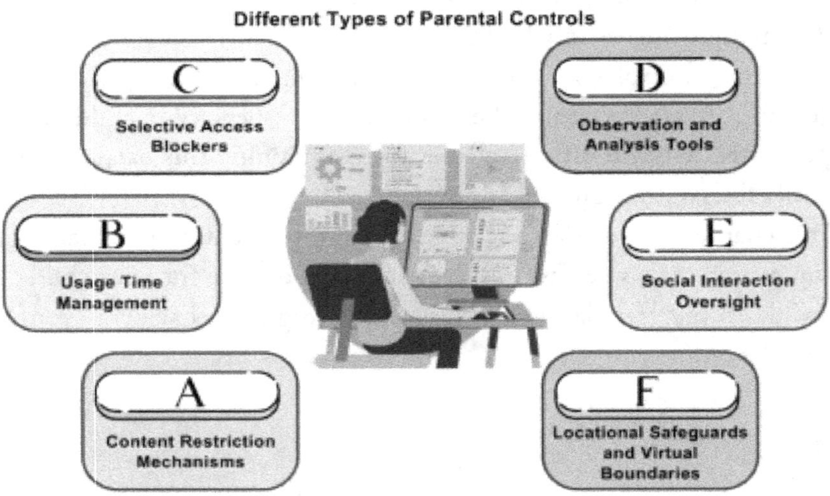

A) Content Restriction Mechanisms

These mechanisms restrict or block access to websites, apps, and media considered inappropriate. They are designed to match your child's age and developmental stage, ensuring they access only suitable material.

- **Internet Filters:** These filters restrict entry to sites with explicit, violent, or inappropriate content by blocking whole categories or specific URLs.
- **Application and Entertainment Filters:** Regulate the type of applications, movies, music, and other media accessible by children, using age ratings and content descriptors as guidelines.

B) Usage Time Management

These tools help parents allocate specific durations for how long children can use digital devices, promoting a balanced lifestyle between the virtual and real world.

- **Time Allocation Limits:** Set precise limits for daily or weekly device usage, which can be defined for various days or specific purposes, like educational activities or entertainment purposes.
- **Sleep Time Controls:** Automatically turn off device access during designated hours to encourage better sleep patterns.

C) Selective Access Blockers

These functionalities permit parents to block access to particular apps or websites they find unsuitable or distracting for their children. This is especially useful during study times or to restrict social media use.

- **Specific App Restrictions:** Allow blocking of apps that are not considered age-appropriate or desired by the parents for their children's use.
- **Selective Web Blocking:** Similar to internet filters, these block access based on the nature of the content or its potential risks.

D) Observation and Analysis Tools

These tools offer detailed feedback on the child's digital behavior by tracking visited sites, used applications, search terms, and time spent online.

- **Digital Footprint Summaries:** Provide overviews of digital engagement, documenting time spent across different platforms and identifying any attempts to breach content restrictions.
- **Instant Alerts:** Send real-time notifications when a child attempts to access prohibited content or displays risky online behavior.

E) Social Interaction Oversight

These tools enable parents to monitor the social exchanges their children engage in online, identifying potential risks like cyberbullying or conversations with unknown individuals.

- **Communication Surveillance:** Some tools allow oversight of messages exchanged on social networks, pinpointing problematic dialogues.
- **Social Profile Oversight:** This service helps parents ensure that their children's social accounts are secured and that interactions remain within safety parameters.

F) Locational Safeguards and Virtual Boundaries

These tools help parents monitor their children's physical whereabouts through digital devices and set up virtual boundaries known as geofencing.

- **Immediate Locational Updates:** Offer real-time data on the child's location, which is instrumental in ensuring their physical safety.
- **Virtual Boundary Settings:** Enable the creation of 'safe zones' like schools or homes, alerting parents if the child crosses these boundaries unexpectedly.

Understanding the scope of parental controls is the initial step towards ensuring a controlled and secure online environment for children. By implementing content restrictions, managing device usage times, blocking inappropriate apps and sites, monitoring digital behaviors, overseeing social interactions, and employing location-based tools, parents can customize their approach to suit their child's needs and uphold family values.

7.2 Setting Up Parental Controls on Various Devices

Setting up parental controls across different devices is essential for ensuring that your child's digital experiences are safe and age-appropriate. Children access the internet through a range of devices, including smartphones, tablets, gaming consoles, and smart TVs, so it is crucial to configure controls on each one. This section guides setting up parental controls on commonly used devices, offering comprehensive protection for your child.

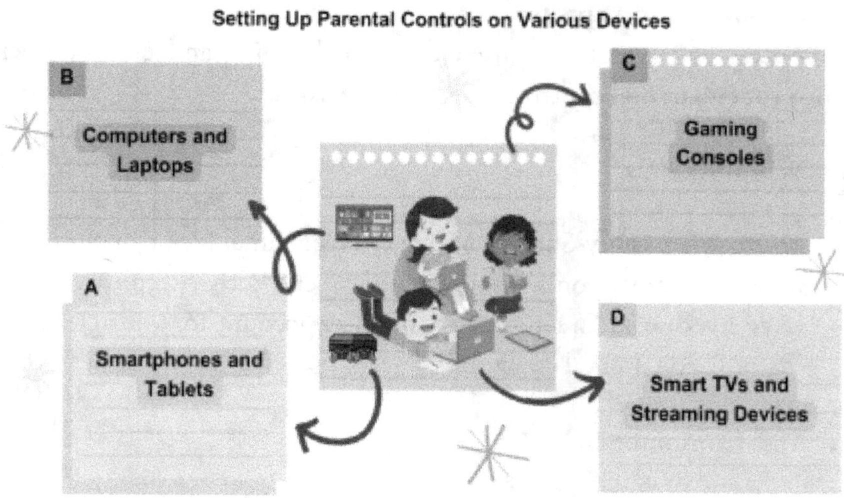

A) Smartphones and Tablets

Smartphones and tablets are widely used by children, making it essential to manage their online activities and screen time.

1. **IOS Devices (iPhone/iPad)**

- **Screen Time:** Set time limits on apps, restrict content, and block specific websites. You can also create a passcode to prevent changes to these settings.
- **Content and Privacy Restrictions:** Block inappropriate content,

restrict purchases, and manage privacy settings, tailoring controls to your child's age.

1. **Android Devices**

- **Google Family Link:** Use this link to manage your child's device remotely, set screen time limits, approve or block app downloads, and monitor activity.
- **Built-in Parental Controls:** Use Android's built-in controls to restrict apps, content, and in-app purchases.

B) Computers and Laptops

Computers and laptops are used for both learning and entertainment, requiring proper parental controls to ensure safe usage.

1. **Windows PCs**

- **Microsoft Family Safety:** Manage screen time, block inappropriate websites, monitor online activity, and receive activity reports.
- **User Accounts:** Create a restricted user account for your child with customized parental controls.

1. **Mac Computers**

- **Screen Time:** Similar to iOS, set app limits, manage content restrictions, and block websites on your child's user account.
- **Content and Privacy Restrictions:** Manage app access, block explicit content, and control in-app purchases.

C) Gaming Consoles

Gaming consoles provide entertainment but can expose children to online interactions and content that may not be suitable.

1. **PlayStation**

- **Family Management:** Create sub-accounts with age-appropriate restrictions, limit communication, and control spending.

- **Time Limits:** Set gameplay time limits to encourage a healthy balance of activities.

1. **Xbox**

- **Xbox Family Settings:** Manage screen time, set content restrictions, and control online interactions with activity monitoring and notifications.
- **App & Content Restrictions:** Restrict access to age-appropriate games, movies, and apps.

1. **Nintendo Switch**

- **Nintendo Parental Controls App:** This app allows users to set playtime limits, restrict games based on age ratings, and monitor gameplay history.
- **Online Interactions:** Limit communication with others online and restrict access to the eShop.

D) Smart TVs and Streaming Devices

Smart TVs and streaming devices provide access to a wide range of content, making it essential to set up parental controls.

1. **Smart TVs**

- **Built-in Parental Controls:** Block specific channels, apps, or content based on ratings, accessible through the TV's settings menu.
- **App Restrictions:** Restrict access to certain apps that may not be appropriate for your child.

1. **Streaming Devices (Roku, Amazon Fire TV, Apple TV)**

- **Parental Controls on Streaming Platforms:** Set up profiles on platforms like Netflix, Hulu, and Disney+ with content appropriate for your child's age.

- **Device Settings:** Use device-level parental controls to restrict access to certain content or apps.

Setting up parental controls on various devices is crucial for creating a secure digital environment for your child. By configuring controls on smartphones, tablets, computers, gaming consoles, and smart TVs, you can ensure that your child's online experiences are safe, age-appropriate, and aligned with your family's values.

7.3 Monitoring and Adjusting Parental Controls Overtime

Setting up parental controls is just the first step in protecting your child online. As they grow and their digital habits change, it is essential to regularly monitor and adjust these controls to ensure they remain effective and appropriate for their age and maturity level. This section highlights the importance of continuous oversight, how to adjust controls as your child develops, and the value of ongoing communication about online safety.

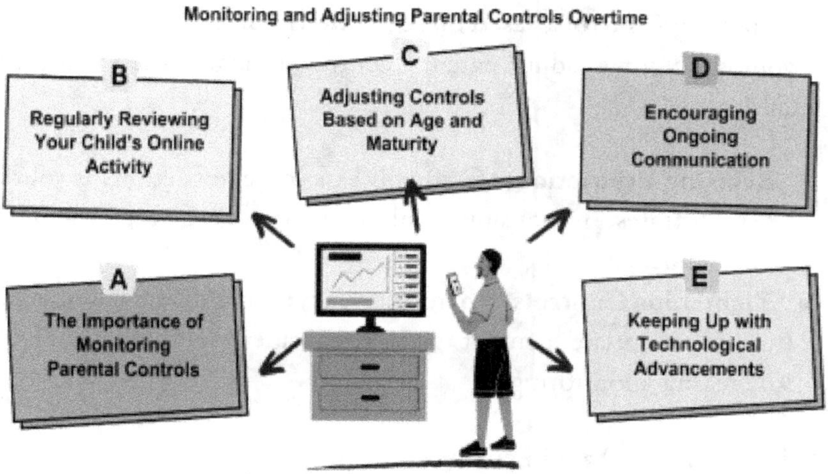

A) The Importance of Monitoring Parental Controls

Parental controls require ongoing monitoring to stay effective. As children mature, their online interests and the associated risks evolve. Regularly reviewing the controls helps ensure they continue to protect your child.

- **Keeping Up with Your Child's Development:** As children's interests expand, controls that were sufficient when they were younger may need adjustment. Monitoring helps you stay ahead of these changes.
- **Responding to New Risks:** The digital landscape is constantly evolving, with new apps and platforms emerging. Regular monitoring allows you to address new risks as they arise.

B) Regularly Reviewing Your Child's Online Activity

Effective monitoring involves keeping track of your child's online activity without violating their privacy.

- **Activity Reports:** Many parental control tools provide reports summarizing your child's online activity, helping you understand their habits and identify potential issues.
- **Behavioral Changes:** Be attentive to changes in behavior, such as secrecy or distress after being online, which may signal the need to adjust controls.

C) Adjusting Controls Based on Age and Maturity

As your child grows, adjust parental controls to match their maturity and responsibility.

- **Relaxing Restrictions:** Gradually ease some restrictions as your child demonstrates responsible online behavior, giving them more independence.
- **Tightening Controls When Necessary:** If risky behavior or exposure to inappropriate content occurs, consider tightening controls or increasing monitoring.

D) Encouraging Ongoing Communication

Regular discussions about online experiences should accompany the monitoring and adjustment of parental controls.

- **Discussing Changes:** Explain the reasons for any adjustments to the controls, whether relaxing or tightening them, to help your child understand their purpose.
- **Listening to Their Concerns:** Encourage your child to share their feelings about the controls and their online experiences, facilitating trust and cooperation.

E) Keeping Up with Technological Advancements

Stay informed about new tools and updates in parental control technology to ensure your child's protection remains current.

- **Updating Tools and Software:** Regularly update parental control tools to benefit from new features and improvements.
- **Exploring New Options:** Be open to trying new solutions that may offer better monitoring flexibility or address emerging online risks.

Monitoring and adjusting parental controls over time is crucial for keeping your child safe in the digital world. By regularly reviewing their activity, adapting controls to their age and maturity, maintaining open communication, and staying updated on technological advancements, you can ensure a dynamic and responsive approach to online safety.

7.4 Using Parental Control Apps and Software

In today's digital landscape, parental control apps and software are essential tools for safeguarding children's online activities. These applications offer a range of features that allow parents to monitor, restrict, and guide their children's internet use, ensuring a safe and controlled digital environment. This section highlights the benefits of using these tools and recommends some of the best options available.

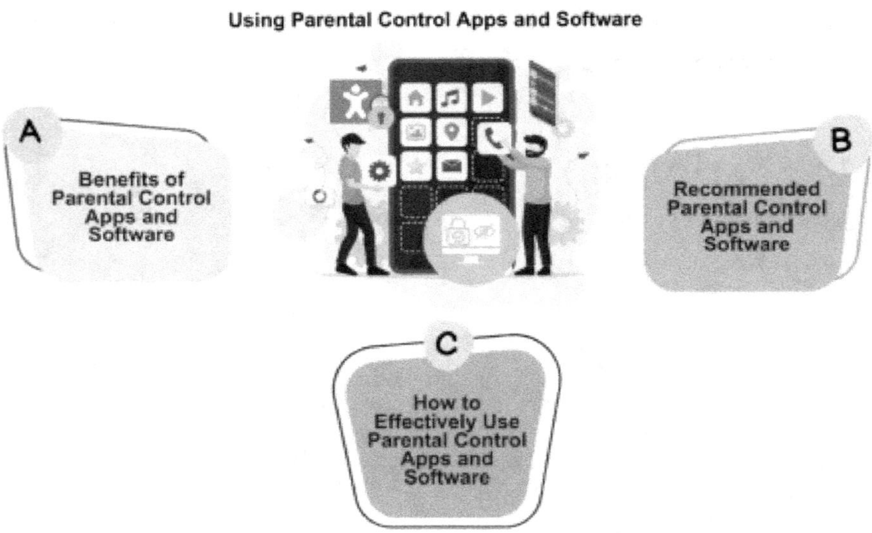

A) The Benefits of Parental Control Apps and Software

Parental control apps and software offer comprehensive solutions for managing your child's online experience, designed to meet your family's specific needs.

- **Comprehensive Monitoring:** These tools allow you to track your child's online activities, including the websites they visit, the apps they use, and their screen time.
- **Content Filtering:** Block access to inappropriate content, ensuring your child encounters only age-appropriate material.

- **Screen Time Management:** Set time limits on device usage to help prevent overuse and encourage a balanced digital diet.
- **Location Tracking:** GPS tracking features help you know your child's whereabouts, providing added safety when they are away from home.
- **Communication Monitoring:** Some apps allow you to monitor text messages, social media interactions, and calls to protect your child from online threats like cyberbullying.

B) Recommended Parental Control Apps and Software

Choosing the right parental control solution depends on your family's needs. Here are some top-rated options:

- **Aura:** It offers robust features, including content filtering, screen time management, location tracking, and identity theft protection. It also provides a dashboard for easy monitoring and real-time alerts.
- **Qustodio:** Known for its ease of use, Qustodio works across multiple devices and offers content filtering, screen time controls, and detailed activity reports, including call and SMS monitoring.
- **Norton Family:** A trusted name in digital security, Norton Family provides tools for web filtering, time management, social media monitoring, and location tracking, with a focus on managing screen time during school hours.
- **Net Nanny:** Offers powerful real-time content filtering, screen time management, and app blocking, with a user-friendly interface and family feed updates on online activity.
- **Bark:** Monitors texts, emails, and social media platforms for signs of harmful behavior, providing detailed reports and alerts on potential issues. Bark also includes web filtering and screen time management.

C) How to Effectively Use Parental Control Apps and Software

To maximize the effectiveness of parental control apps and software:

- **Customize Settings:** You can customize the settings based on your child's age and maturity level. Younger children may need stricter controls, while older children might benefit from more flexibility.

- **Review Activity Regularly:** Check the reports and alerts provided by the app regularly to stay informed about your child's online behavior.
- **Communicate with Your Child:** Use the information gathered to discuss your child's online activities, explaining the reasons behind the restrictions and encouraging open dialogue.
- **Update and Adjust:** As your child grows, update and adjust the settings to reflect their changing needs and the evolving digital landscape.

Parental control apps and software are invaluable tools for managing your child's online safety. Solutions like Aura, Qustodio, Norton Family, Net Nanny, and Bark help you monitor activities, set boundaries, and protect your child from digital threats. However, these tools are most effective when combined with ongoing communication and education about online safety.

7.5 Educating Kids about Parental Controls

While parental controls are vital for safeguarding children's online activities, it is equally important to educate them on why these controls are in place and how they contribute to their online safety. Educating children about parental controls not only promotes understanding but also encourages them to take an active role in their digital safety. This section explores how to explain parental controls to children and how to enable a collaborative approach to online safety.

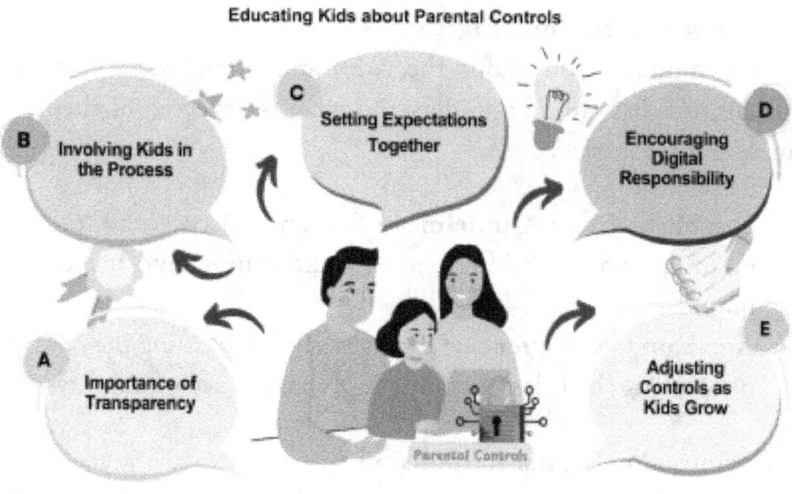

A) The Importance of Transparency

Being open about parental controls is crucial for building trust and helping children understand that these measures are meant to protect them, not violate their privacy.

- **Explain the Purpose:** Clarify that parental controls are there to keep them safe from harmful content and online risks, much like a seatbelt in a car.
- **Discuss the Benefits:** Highlight how these controls help block inappropriate content, set healthy screen time limits, and prevent online scams.

B) Involving Kids in the Process

Involving your children in setting up and managing parental controls can make them feel more comfortable and responsible for their online safety.

- **Invite Their Input:** Ask for their opinions on which apps or websites to restrict and set limits together, making them feel involved and valued.
- **Educate them on How Controls Work:** Show them how the controls function so they understand the mechanics behind their digital protection.

C) Setting Expectations Together

Clear communication about the rules and boundaries set by parental controls ensures that children understand what is expected of them and why these measures are in place.

- **Establish Clear Guidelines:** Set and discuss the rules openly, ensuring your children understand the importance of these boundaries.
- **Agree on Consequences:** Involve them in deciding the consequences of breaking the rules, encouraging a sense of accountability.

D) Encouraging Digital Responsibility

As children mature, encourage them to take more responsibility for their online safety, promoting digital literacy and responsible behavior.

- **Promote Self-Regulation:** Encourage them to self-regulate activities like screen time, teaching discipline and healthy digital habits.
- **Discuss Online Safety Regularly:** Keep online safety a regular conversation topic, reinforcing the importance of responsible behavior.

E) Adjusting Controls as Kids Grow

As children demonstrate responsible online behavior, consider gradually relaxing parental controls to grant them more freedom, reward their maturity, and build their confidence.

- **Gradual Relaxation of Controls:** Adjust controls as they grow, allowing more freedom while still ensuring safety.
- **Continuous Learning and Adaptation:** Encourage ongoing learning about online risks, adapting controls to match their growing understanding and independence.

Educating kids about parental controls is critical to facilitating a safe and healthy digital environment. By being transparent, involving them in the process, setting clear expectations, and encouraging digital responsibility, parents can help their children understand and appreciate the importance of these measures.

7.6 Balancing Control and Trust

Finding the right balance between control and trust is a key challenge in digital parenting. While parental controls are necessary for your child's safety, they should be implemented in a way that respects their growing need for independence and privacy. This section explores how to strike that balance, ensuring your child feels supported and protected without being overly restricted.

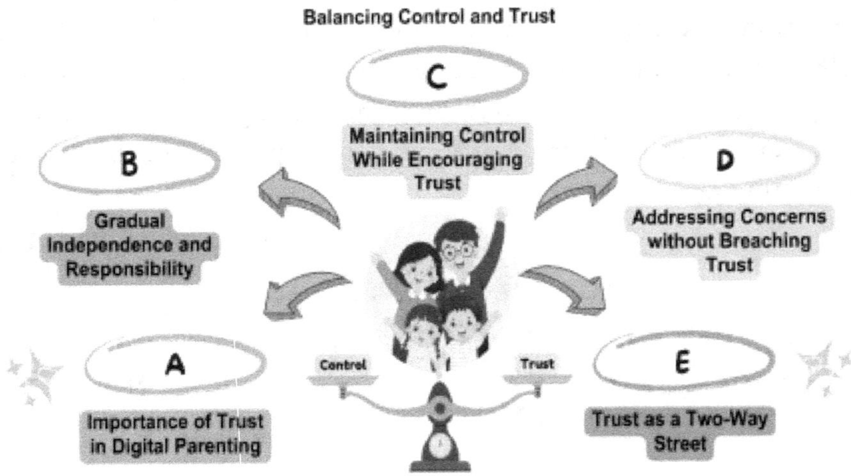

A) The Importance of Trust in Digital Parenting

Trust is the cornerstone of managing your child's online activities. When children feel trusted, they are more likely to be open about their online experiences and less likely to engage in risky behavior.

- **Building Trust through Transparency:** Be open about why you have set up parental controls. When children understand these measures are for their protection, they are more likely to accept them.
- **Promoting Open Communication:** Encourage your child to discuss their online experiences, building trust and addressing concerns before they become issues.

B) Gradual Independence and Responsibility

As children grow, they seek more independence. Gradually loosening controls and giving them more responsibility helps them explore the digital world safely on their own.

- **Easing Restrictions Overtime:** As your child shows responsible behavior, consider gradually easing controls, demonstrating trust in their judgment.
- **Encouraging Self-Regulation:** Teach your child to self-regulate screen time and content choices, preparing them for greater independence.

C) Maintaining Control While Encouraging Trust

It is important to maintain some control while respecting your child's freedom. Implement controls that support their growing independence.

- **Collaborative Rule Setting:** Involve your child in setting online behavior rules, which will make them more likely to follow the guidelines they helped create.
- **Regular Check-Ins:** Conduct regular, non-intrusive check-ins to stay informed without constantly monitoring, reinforcing trust.

D) Addressing Concerns without Breaching Trust

When concerns arise, address them carefully to avoid damaging the trust you have built.

- **Approach with Empathy:** Discuss concerns with understanding, focusing on learning rather than punishment.
- **Focus on Education:** Use these moments to educate about online risks, helping your child learn and grow.

E) Trust as a Two-Way Street

Building trust is mutual. Show your child that you trust them by acknowledging their good decisions and gradually increasing their online freedom.

- **Recognize Good Choices:** Praise responsible online behavior, reinforcing their sense of responsibility.
- **Gradually Increase Freedom:** As your child demonstrates trustworthiness, increase their online independence, showing trust is earned and respected.

Balancing control and trust is essential in digital parenting. By maintaining transparency, encouraging open communication, and gradually increasing your child's independence, you can protect them while encouraging a trusting and respectful relationship. In this chapter, we have explored the importance of implementing and managing parental controls to create a safe digital environment for your child. By balancing control with trust, and adapting these measures as your child grows, you ensure their online safety while fostering a sense of responsibility and independence. In the next chapter, we will discuss the benefits of active participation in your child's online life, showing how your engagement can further enhance their safety and support positive digital experiences.

Chapter 8: Active Participation in Kid's Online Lives

In today's digital world, active parental involvement in children's online experiences is crucial. While setting up parental controls and establishing rules is essential, being engaged in your child's digital activities allows you to guide, support, and teach them in real-time. This chapter explores practical ways to be involved, ensuring that your child stays safe while making responsible and positive choices online.

Co-Playing Online Games

Co-playing online games with your child offers a valuable opportunity to bond, monitor content, and discuss online safety and etiquette. It is a fun and effective way to stay connected to your child's interests and guide their gaming habits.

Supervising Online Interactions

As children increasingly interact online, it is essential to supervise their communications. By staying involved, you can help them explore social dynamics, recognize potential dangers, and develop healthy online relationships.

Encouraging Positive Online Behaviors

Promoting positive online behaviors helps your child become a responsible digital citizen. Encourage kindness, respect, and thoughtful communication, setting clear expectations for how they should interact online.

Discussing Online Content Together

Discussing online content helps your child critically evaluate what they encounter on the internet. These conversations allow you to address concerns, reinforce safe practices, and help your child make informed decisions.

Being a Role Model for Healthy Digital Habits

Children learn from observing their parents. By modelling balanced technology use and responsible online behavior, you set a strong example for your child to follow, helping them develop a positive relationship with technology.

Active participation in your child's online life is about more than just monitoring; it is about engaging with them, guiding their behavior, and encouraging open communication. This chapter provides strategies to help you be a proactive and supportive presence in your child's digital world, ensuring they explore the internet safely and responsibly.

8.1 Co-Playing Online Games / Playing Online Games Together

Playing online games with your children is a valuable opportunity to be actively involved in their digital lives. Not only does it allow you to understand the games they are playing, but it also helps you build a stronger bond with them while ensuring that they engage in safe and age-appropriate activities. This section explores the benefits of co-gaming and offers practical tips on how to make the most of these shared experiences.

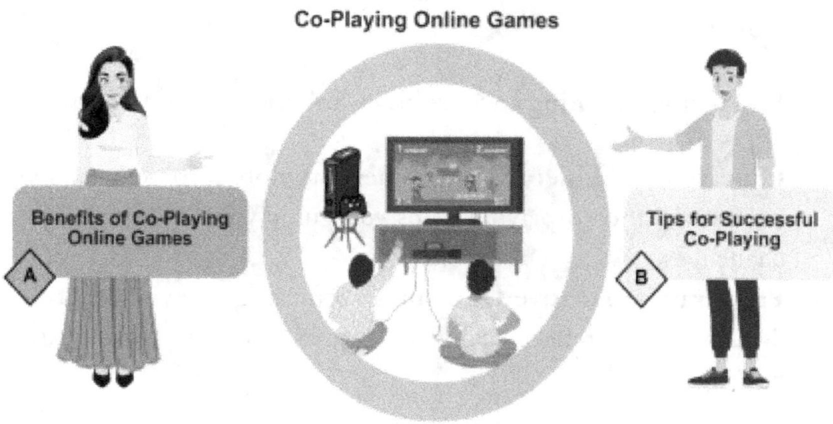

A) Benefits of Shared Online Games

1. **Building Trust and Communication**

- **Strengthening Relationships:** Playing together enables open communication and a deeper connection through shared interests.
- **Understanding Interests:** By participating, you gain insight into your child's hobbies, leading to more meaningful conversations about their online interactions.

1. **Monitoring Content and Behavior**

- **Assessing Game Content:** Co-gaming allows you to directly observe the game's content, ensuring it is appropriate for your child's age.

- **Observing Online Interactions:** You can monitor social interactions within the game, teaching your child how to handle inappropriate behavior.

1. **Teaching Digital Etiquette**

- **Modelling Good Behavior:** You can demonstrate respectful online behavior, setting a positive example for your child.
- **Discussing Online Conduct:** Use gameplay moments to discuss the importance of kindness, privacy, and the impact of their actions online.

1. **Enhancing Learning and Problem-Solving**

- **Educational Value:** Many games promote problem-solving and teamwork, and co-playing helps you guide your child through these challenges.
- **Encouraging Positive Outcomes:** You can guide your child toward decisions that reflect real-world values, such as cooperation and patience.

B) Tips for Successful Co-Playing

1. **Choose the Right Games**

- **Age-Appropriate:** Select games suitable for your child's age and that promote positive interactions.
- **Collaborative:** Choose games that encourage teamwork, reinforcing the value of cooperation.

1. **Set Boundaries and Expectations**

- **Game Time Limits:** Agree on how long you will play together and maintain a healthy balance with offline activities.
- **Discuss Game Rules:** Set guidelines for behavior, emphasizing

respect and positive conduct.

1. **Engage in Post-Game Discussions**

- **Reflect on the Experience:** Talk about what your child enjoyed and learned, reinforcing the lessons from gameplay.
- **Address Concerns:** Calmly discuss any troubling behavior or content, using it as a teaching moment.

Co-gaming is an effective way to stay connected to your child's digital world, ensuring their safety while promoting positive habits. Through active participation, you can build trust, monitor content, teach digital etiquette, and enhance their learning.

8.2 Supervising Online Interactions

Supervising your child's online interactions is a crucial aspect of ensuring their safety in the digital world. As children engage in social media, messaging apps, and online gaming, they are exposed to various forms of communication that can be both positive and negative. Active supervision allows parents to guide their children's interactions, helping them explore online relationships responsibly and safely. This section will discuss the importance of supervising online interactions, the potential risks involved, and practical strategies for adequate supervision.

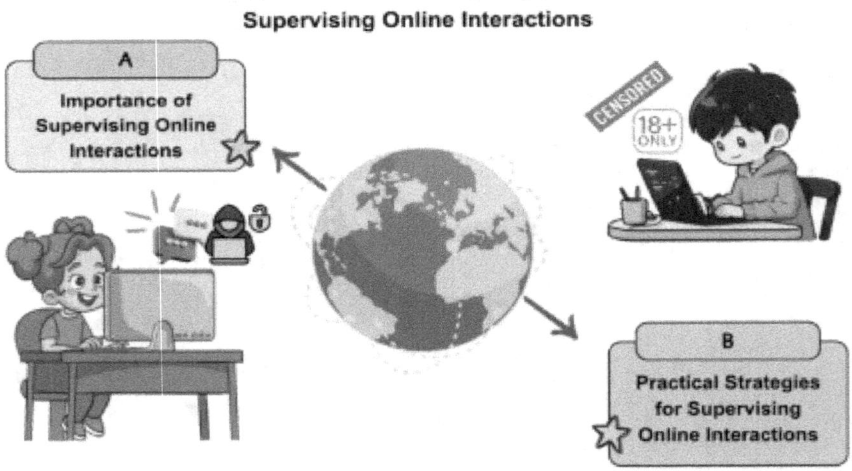

A) Importance of Supervising Online Interactions

1. **Protecting Against Online Risks**

- **Exposure to Inappropriate Content:** Supervision helps prevent children from encountering harmful language, explicit images, or discussions that are not age-appropriate.
- **Preventing Cyberbullying:** Early identification of cyberbullying through supervision allows for timely intervention and support.
- **Avoiding Online Predators:** By monitoring interactions, parents can

protect their children from engaging with suspicious or dangerous individuals.

1. **Encouraging Positive Online Behavior**

- **Teaching Digital Etiquette:** Supervision provides opportunities to teach respect, privacy, and positive communication online.
- **Guiding Responsible Communication:** Parents can help children make wise decisions about what they share and how they interact in digital spaces.

1. **Building Trust and Communication**

- **Open Dialogue:** Supervision should be framed as a safety measure, encouraging openness rather than fear.
- **Supportive Environment:** Being involved allows parents to offer support when children encounter challenges online.

B) Practical Strategies for Supervising Online Interactions

1. **Use of Parental Control Tools**

- **Activity Monitoring:** Parental control tools can provide insights into your child's online activities, including who they communicate with and what they share.
- **Content Filtering:** Set filters to block inappropriate content and restrict access to unsuitable websites or apps.

1. **Regular Check-Ins**

- **Reviewing Communication:** Periodically review your child's online communications with their knowledge, explaining that this is necessary for their safety.
- **Discussing Online Interactions:** Regularly talk about their online experiences, friends, and any uncomfortable situations they encounter.

1. **Setting Clear Boundaries**

- **Rules for Online Communication:** Establish and explain rules for online behavior, including not sharing personal information and avoiding negative interactions.
- **Time Limits:** Set limits on time spent online, encouraging a balance with offline activities.

1. **Encouraging Responsible Online Relationships**

- **Choosing Trusted Contacts:** Encourage your child to interact only with people they know and trust in real life.
- **Discussing the Impact of Words:** Teach them to think before posting or sending messages, promoting kindness and respect.

1. **Modelling Positive Behavior**

- **Lead by Example:** Demonstrate positive online behavior in your digital interactions.
- **Sharing Experiences:** Share your own experiences with online communication to provide valuable lessons.

Supervising your child's online interactions is not just a safety measure but a crucial step in promoting responsible digital habits. By using parental control tools, setting clear boundaries, and maintaining open communication, you can guide your child through the complexities of online relationships. This not only protects them from potential dangers but also helps them interact positively and safely in the digital world.

8.3 Encouraging Positive Online Behaviors

In today's digital world, guiding children to develop positive online behaviors is essential. These behaviors not only protect them from online risks but also contribute to a respectful and supportive digital community. This section highlights the importance of encouraging positive online conduct and offers practical strategies for parents to help their children become responsible digital citizens.

A) The Importance of Positive Online Behaviors

1. **Building a Respectful Digital Presence**

- **Impact on Others:** Encouraging kindness and respect in online interactions helps create a safer, more welcoming environment for everyone.
- **Preventing Cyberbullying:** Teaching children the value of treating others with respect reduces the likelihood of them engaging in or tolerating cyberbullying.

1. **Protecting Personal Reputation**

- **Long-Term Consequences:** Instilling the habit of thinking before posting helps children avoid damaging their reputations.
- **Digital Footprint Awareness:** Educating children about their digital footprint encourages them to maintain a positive online identity.

1. **Promoting Safe Online Practices**

- **Avoiding Risky Behaviors:** Positive behaviors, such as avoiding oversharing and staying away from harmful websites, result in safer digital experiences.

B) Strategies for Encouraging Positive Online Behaviors

1. **Modeling Good Behavior**

- **Lead by Example:** Demonstrate respectful and responsible online behavior for your child to imitate.
- **Sharing Experiences:** Discuss how you handle online challenges with calmness and respect.

1. **Teaching Empathy and Respect**

- **Understanding other's Perspectives:** Help your child consider the impact of their words and actions on others.
- **Encouraging Kindness:** Promote kindness in online interactions and the importance of supporting others.

1. **Setting Clear Expectations**

- **Establishing Rules for Online Behavior:** Define clear guidelines for respectful and honest online communication.
- **Discussing Consequences:** Explain the real-world effects of negative online behavior on both themselves and others.

1. **Promoting Positive Content Creation**

- **Encouraging Creativity:** Support your child in using the internet to share positive and creative content.
- **Highlighting Good Role Models:** Point out positive online figures who exemplify the behaviors you want your child to follow.

1. **Reinforcing Positive Behavior**

- **Praise and Recognition:** Acknowledge and reward your child when they demonstrate positive online behavior.
- **Rewarding Good Practices:** Consider small rewards for consistently displaying good digital citizenship.

1. **Encouraging Critical Thinking**

- **Questioning Online Content:** Teach your child to evaluate the credibility of online information and avoid spreading misinformation.
- **Evaluating Societal Pressure:** Help them build the confidence to make positive choices, even under societal pressure.

Encouraging positive online behaviors is crucial for helping children become responsible and respectful digital citizens. By modelling good behavior, teaching empathy, setting clear expectations, and promoting positive content, parents can guide their children toward making thoughtful and safe choices online.

8.4 Discussing Online Content Together

Engaging in discussions about the online content your child encounters is essential for guiding them through the complexities of the digital world. By talking openly about what they see, please read, and experience online, you help them develop critical thinking skills, make informed decisions, and stay safe. This section highlights the importance of discussing online content together and provides practical strategies for meaningful conversations.

A) The Importance of Discussing Online Content

1. **Enhancing Critical Thinking**

- **Evaluating Information:** Discussing online content helps children learn to assess the credibility of the information they encounter, distinguishing between reliable sources and misinformation.
- **Recognizing Bias:** Conversations about online content can help children identify bias and develop a more balanced understanding of the issues they encounter.

1. **Promoting Safe Online Practices**

- **Identifying Inappropriate Content:** Talking about what they see online helps children recognize and avoid inappropriate or harmful material.
- **Preventing Risky Behavior:** Regular discussions reinforce the importance of safe online practices, such as not sharing personal information or avoiding suspicious links.

1. **Strengthening Parent-Child Relationships**

- **Building Trust and Openness:** Engaging with your child about their online experiences facilitates trust and openness, encouraging them to share and seek guidance.
- **Supporting Emotional Well-being:** Discussing online content allows you to support your child emotionally, helping them process what they see or read.

B) Strategies for Discussing Online Content

1. **Create a Comfortable Environment**

- **Open-Ended Questions:** Ask open-ended questions to encourage your child to share more about their online experiences.
- **Non-Judgmental Listening:** Listen without judgment, even if they have encountered something inappropriate, using the moment as a learning opportunity.

1. **Regularly Check-In**

- **Daily or Weekly Conversations:** Make discussions about online content a regular part of your routine, ensuring your child feels comfortable sharing.
- **Use Current Events as Starters:** Discuss current events or popular trends as a way to start conversations about online content.

1. **Guide Critical Thinking**

- **Ask for Their Opinion:** Encourage your child to share their opinions and think critically about the content they encounter.
- **Explore the Source:** Together, evaluate the source of online content to teach your child how to assess its reliability.

1. **Address Sensitive Topics**

- **Handle with Care:** Approach sensitive topics with honesty and age-appropriate explanations while reinforcing family values.
- **Reinforce Family Values:** Use these discussions to align content with your family's values, helping your child understand why understanding is essential.

1. **Encourage Positive Content Exploration**

- **Highlight Educational Resources:** Encourage exploration of positive and educational content, broadening their thinking.
- **Celebrate Positive Discoveries:** Celebrate when your child finds positive content online, reinforcing the value of sharing and seeking out beneficial material.

Discussing online content with your child is a powerful way to guide them through the digital world, encouraging critical thinking and safe online practices. By creating a comfortable environment for open dialogue, regularly checking in, and guiding their exploration, you help your child become a thoughtful and discerning digital citizen.

8.5 Being a Role Model for Healthy Digital Habits

In the digital age, children often look to their parents for guidance on how to navigate the online world. Being a role model for healthy digital habits is one of the most effective ways to teach your child responsible internet use. By demonstrating positive online behavior, setting boundaries, and maintaining a healthy relationship with technology, you can help your child develop similar habits that will benefit them throughout their lives. This section explores the importance of being a digital role model and offers practical tips for setting a positive example.

A) The Importance of Modeling Healthy Digital Habits

1. Children Imitate Parental Behavior

- **Learning through Observation:** Children learn by observing their parents. When they see you using technology responsibly, they are more likely to adopt similar behaviors.
- **Establishing Norms:** By modelling healthy digital habits, you establish norms for how technology should be used within your household.

1. **Promoting Balance and Well-Being**

- **Encouraging a Balanced Lifestyle:** Demonstrating a balanced approach to technology encourages your child to engage in offline activities, promoting overall well-being.
- **Reducing Screen Time Dependency:** When children see their parents managing screen time effectively, they are less likely to develop unhealthy dependencies on digital devices.

1. **Encouraging Digital Responsibility**

- **Setting Standards for Online Behavior:** Your online behavior serves as a blueprint for how your child should conduct themselves on the internet.
- **Highlighting Privacy and Security:** Modeling good habits around privacy and security reinforces these critical aspects of online safety.

B) Strategies for Being a Positive Digital Role Model

1. **Demonstrate Balanced Technology Use**

- **Set Screen Time Limits for Yourself:** Show your child that even adults need to limit screen time, emphasizing the importance of balance.
- **Prioritize Family Time:** Make family time a priority by setting aside devices during meals and conversations and teaching that technology should not interfere with personal interactions.

1. **Practice What You Preach**

- **Follow the Rules You Set:** If you set screen time rules for your child, follow similar guidelines yourself to reinforce the importance of these rules.
- **Be Mindful of Your Online Presence:** Ensure that your social media activity aligns with the values that you want in your child.

1. **Engage in Positive Online Activities**

- **Use Technology for Good:** Demonstrate how technology can be used positively, such as learning new skills or connecting meaningfully with others.
- **Share Positive Content:** Share inspiring or educational content with your child, encouraging them to seek out and share positive material.

1. **Teach Digital Etiquette and Safety**

- **Discuss Your Online Choices:** Talk to your child about your online decisions to help them understand the importance of digital etiquette and safety.
- **Involve Them in Security Practices:** Show your child how you protect your devices and personal information, reinforcing the importance of online security.

1. **Encourage Open Communication**

- **Be Open About Your Online Experiences:** Share your online experiences to encourage your child to do the same, enabling trust.
- **Discuss the Impact of Technology:** Regularly talk about how technology affects daily life, helping your child develop a critical awareness of their digital habits.

Being a role model for healthy digital habits is crucial in shaping your child's relationship with technology. By demonstrating balance, practicing what you preach, engaging in positive online activities, and maintaining open communication, you set the stage for your child to develop responsible and healthy digital habits. Active participation in your child's online life is essential for facilitating a safe and positive digital experience. By co-playing games, supervising online interactions, encouraging positive behaviors, discussing content together, and being a role model for healthy digital habits, you create a supportive environment that helps your child navigate the digital world with confidence and responsibility. As we move forward, the next chapter will guide you through the crucial steps to take if you suspect online issues, ensuring that you are prepared to address any challenges that may arise in your child's digital journey.

Chapter 9: Steps to Take if You Suspect Online Issues

As children explore the digital world, they may encounter challenges that can impact their well-being and safety. In today's connected society, it is increasingly important for parents to be vigilant and proactive in recognizing and addressing these issues. This chapter provides a comprehensive guide for parents on how to take appropriate and timely action if they suspect their child is facing online problems, ensuring that they are well-equipped to support and protect their children in the digital age.

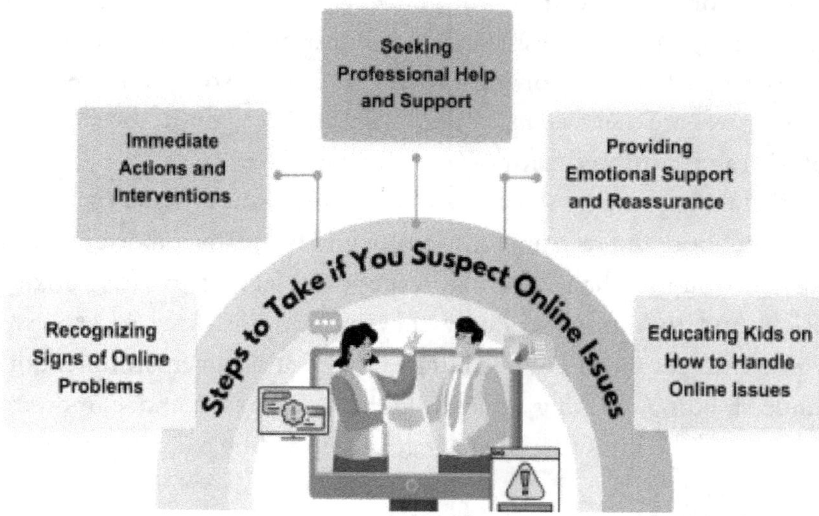

Recognizing Signs of Online Problems

Understanding the early warning signs that may indicate your child is struggling with online issues is the first critical step in providing the help they need. By paying close attention to changes in behavior, mood, and online habits, parents can identify potential problems before they escalate. This section will discuss common indicators of online distress, such as sudden mood swings, changes in social behavior, and physical symptoms like sleep disturbances, helping parents to recognize when something is wrong.

Immediate Actions and Interventions

Once a potential issue is identified, knowing how to respond quickly and effectively is crucial. Immediate intervention can prevent further harm and start the process of resolving the problem. This section will outline practical steps that parents can take, from adjusting privacy settings and blocking harmful contacts to directly engaging with their child to understand the situation better. It emphasizes the importance of staying calm, gathering information, and taking protective measures to ensure the child's safety.

Seeking Professional Help and Support

In some instances, the challenges children face online may be too complex or severe to handle alone. Professional help may be necessary to address issues such as severe cyberbullying, exposure to harmful content, or interactions with online predators. This section will guide when to seek additional support, including counselling, legal assistance, or educational intervention. It will also explain the benefits of involving experts to ensure your child receives the comprehensive care they need.

Providing Emotional Support and Reassurance

While taking practical steps to address online issues is essential, providing emotional support and reassurance to your child is equally important. Children dealing with online challenges may experience feelings of fear, anxiety, or confusion, and they need to know they have a safe space to express their emotions. This section will offer strategies for creating an environment of trust and understanding, helping your child feel supported and empowered to overcome the difficulties they are facing, and providing parents with a sense of peace of mind.

Educating Kids on How to Handle Online Issues

Empowering children with the knowledge and skills to manage online challenges on their own is vital to their long-term digital well-being. As they grow and become more independent, they must understand how to explore the digital world safely and responsibly. This final section will provide practical tips for educating children about online safety, from recognizing and avoiding risks to responding appropriately when issues arise. By equipping them with these skills, parents can help their children build confidence and strength in the face of online challenges and feel empowered in their role as digital mentors.

By following the steps outlined in this chapter, parents can effectively identify and resolve online challenges, ensuring their child's safety and emotional well-being in the digital world. These proactive measures also help establish a foundation of trust and open communication, enabling a positive and supportive relationship between parents and children as they journey through the complexities of the digital landscape.

9.1 Recognizing Signs of Online Problems

As children become more engaged with the digital world, parents must stay alert to potential signs of online issues. Early recognition of these signs can prevent problems from escalating and allow for timely intervention. This section highlights common indicators that may suggest your child is facing online difficulties and how to respond effectively.

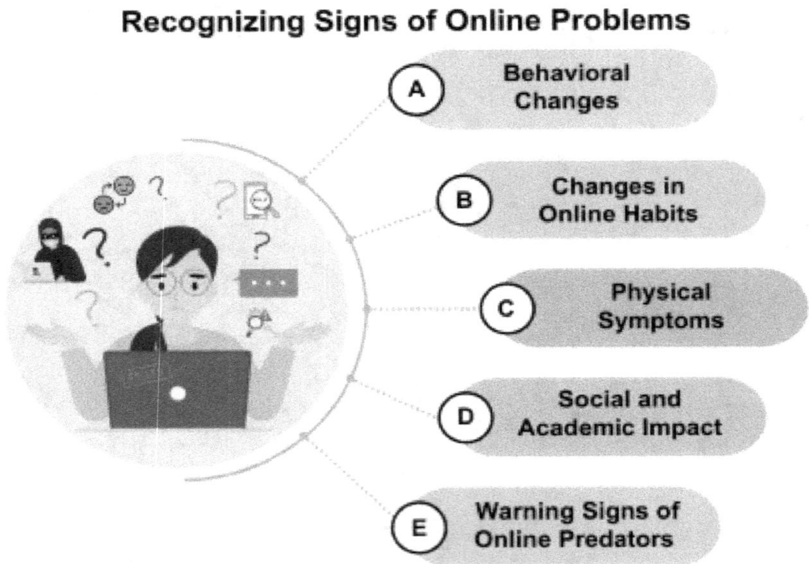

A) Behavioral Changes

- **Mood Swings:** Noticeable irritability, withdrawal, or increased anxiety after using devices may signal negative online experiences like cyberbullying or exposure to harmful content.
- **Avoidance:** Evasive behavior when discussing online activities or hiding screens could indicate that they are encountering something troubling.

B) Changes in Online Habits

- **Excessive Screen Time:** A significant increase in time spent online, particularly late at night, might point to digital addiction or unhealthy online interactions.
- **New or Unfamiliar Apps:** Sudden use of unknown apps or frequent account changes can be red flags for risky online behavior.

C) Physical Symptoms

- **Sleep Issues:** Trouble sleeping, nightmares, or constant fatigue may result from late-night screen use or distressing online experiences.
- **Physical Complaints:** Headaches, eye strain, or posture problems could indicate excessive or unhealthy device usage.

D) Social and Academic Impact

- **Withdrawal from Activities:** Loss of interest in socializing or a decline in social skills may suggest an overreliance on digital interactions.
- **Academic Decline:** Falling grades or poor concentration could be linked to distractions or stress from online activities.

E) Warning Signs of Online Predators or Cyberbullying

- **Secretive Behavior:** Receiving strange messages, unexplained expenses, or a sudden hesitancy to go online may indicate interaction with an online predator or cyberbullying.
- **Manipulation Indicators:** Sudden changes in friendships or unexplained purchases suggest your child is being manipulated online.

Recognizing the signs of online problems is essential for protecting your child from digital dangers. By staying vigilant and noticing changes in behavior, online habits, and overall well-being, parents can take early action to address these issues and ensure their child's safety.

9.2 Immediate Actions and Interventions

When you suspect your child is facing online issues like cyberbullying, exposure to inappropriate content, or interactions with an online predator, taking swift and appropriate action is crucial. Immediate intervention can mitigate the problem, protect your child from further harm, and begin the process of resolution. This section outlines the immediate steps parents should take to address potential online problems and safeguard their child's well-being.

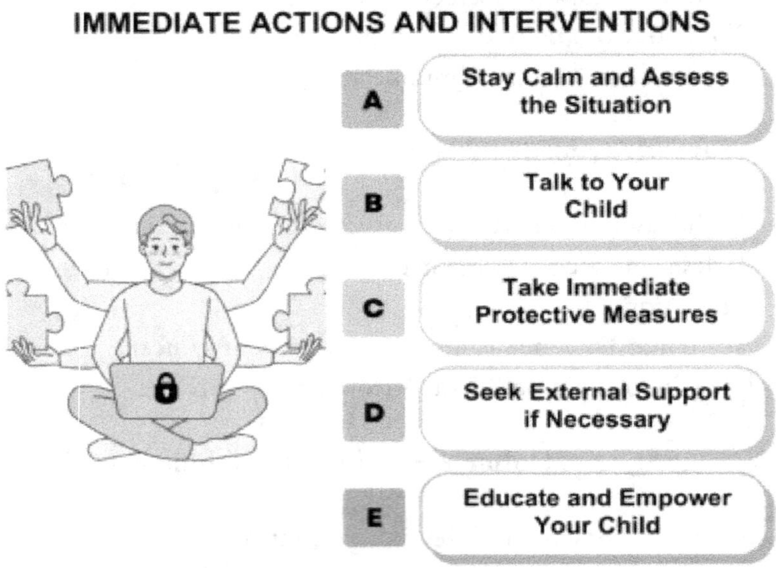

A) Stay Calm and Assess the Situation

- **Remain Composed:** Avoid panicking, which could cause your child to become uncommunicative. Instead, gather information calmly and create an environment where your child feels safe sharing what happened.
- **Evaluate the Severity:** Determine the risk level and whether external intervention is necessary. Document any relevant evidence, such as screenshots, for potential reporting.

B) Talk to Your Child

- **Create a Safe Space:** Approach your child with empathy, encouraging open discussion without judgment. Listen to their experience and provide emotional support.
- **Reassure and Support:** Let your child know they are not alone. To help them feel more in control, involve them in deciding the following steps, such as blocking someone or reporting an issue.

C) Take Immediate Protective Measures

- **Adjust Privacy Settings:** Enhance privacy controls on your child's devices and social media accounts. Block or report offenders to prevent further contact.
- **Limit Online Access Temporarily:** Depending on the severity of the situation, consider reducing your child's online activity temporarily to give them time to recover and prevent further harm.

D) Seek External Support if Necessary

- **Involve School Authorities:** If the issue involves cyberbullying or affects school life, inform the school and work together on a plan to ensure your child's safety.
- **Contact Law Enforcement:** In cases of serious threats or contact with potential predators, involve law enforcement immediately and provide them with any documentation you have gathered.
- **Seek Professional Counseling:** If your child is struggling emotionally, consider professional counselling to help them process their feelings and build resilience.

E) Educate and Empower Your Child

- **Review Online Safety Practices:** After the immediate crisis, reinforce online safety rules with your child, empowering them with knowledge and tools to protect themselves in the future.
- **Build Confidence and Resilience:** Encourage your child to move

forward, focusing on positive online experiences and helping them regain confidence in their digital interactions.

Quick and thoughtful intervention is critical to protecting your child when online issues arise. By staying calm, talking to your child, taking protective measures, seeking external support, and educating them about online safety, you can help them navigate the situation and emerge stronger.

9.3 Seeking Professional Help and Support

When dealing with significant online issues like severe cyberbullying, exposure to harmful content, or interactions with online predators, seeking professional help is crucial. Professional support offers the expertise needed to address complex challenges, protect your child's well-being, and effectively resolve the situation. This section outlines when and how to seek professional help, the types of support available, and the benefits of involving experts in your child's digital safety.

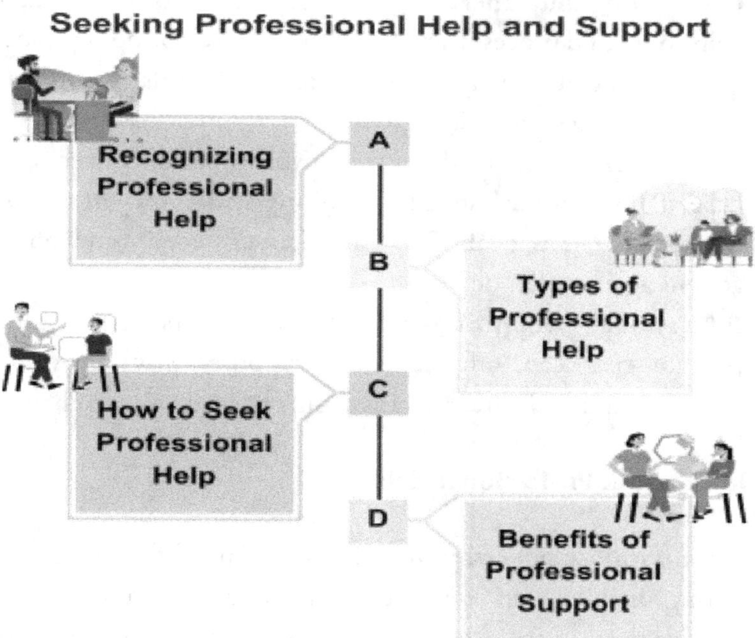

A) Recognizing Professional Help

- **Signs of Emotional Distress:** Significant changes in behavior, mood swings, or physical symptoms like headaches or trouble sleeping can indicate that your child is struggling with online issues. If these signs persist, professional counselling may be necessary.
- **Escalating Online Threats:** If cyberbullying becomes severe or if an

online predator contacts your child, it is time to seek external help. Legal and emotional support from professionals is essential in these situations.

- **Difficulty Managing the Situation:** If the situation feels overwhelming or beyond your ability to manage, professional guidance can provide clarity and support in guiding the legal, emotional, and practical aspects of the issue.

B) Types of Professional Help and Support

- **Counselling and Therapy:** Child psychologists and therapists can help your child process their experiences, develop coping mechanisms, and recover emotionally. Family counselling can also provide strategies for supporting your child at home.
- **Legal Assistance:** If the issue involves legal concerns, such as cyberstalking or harassment, consulting an attorney or involving law enforcement is critical. They can offer protection and pursue legal actions against offenders.
- **Educational Support:** School counsellors and educational psychologists can offer essential support, ensuring your child's academic and social life remains positive despite online challenges.

C) How to Seek Professional Help

- **Start with a Conversation:** Discuss the need for professional help with your child, emphasizing that it is about support, not punishment. Involve them in the process of choosing a professional to ensure their comfort and willingness to participate.
- **Finding the Right Professional:** Research professionals specializing in child psychology, internet law, or relevant fields. Seek recommendations from trusted sources, and ensure the professional's credentials and experience align with your child's needs.
- **Making the First Appointment:** Prepare for the first meeting by gathering relevant information and encouraging your child to be open. This preparation helps the professional provide adequate support

from the start.

D) The Benefits of Professional Support

- **Emotional Healing and Recovery:** Professional counselling provides a safe space for your child to process their experiences, build resilience, and develop coping strategies for future challenges.
- **Legal Protection and Resolution:** Legal professionals ensure your child's safety by taking appropriate legal action against offenders and helping to resolve the issue effectively.
- **Educational and Social Support:** School counsellors and educational psychologists help maintain a positive school experience and improve your child's social skills, ensuring they manage online and offline interactions confidently.

Seeking professional help is vital when facing significant online issues. Whether through counselling, legal assistance, or educational support, involving experts ensures your child receives the care and protection they need.

9.4 Providing Emotional Support and Reassurance

When children face online issues such as cyberbullying or exposure to harmful content, they often experience intense emotions like fear and anxiety. As a parent, providing emotional support and reassurance is crucial to help them handle these challenges and regain their sense of security. This section explores how to offer the necessary emotional support during difficult times, helping your child feel understood, safe, and empowered to overcome these challenges.

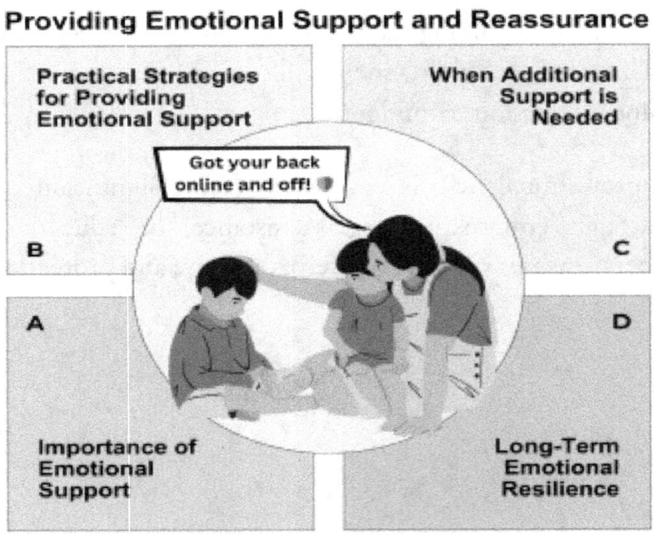

A) The Importance of Emotional Support

- **Building Trust and Openness:** Creating a safe space encourages your child to share their fears without judgment, strengthening the parent-child bond and ensuring they feel secure in seeking your guidance.
- **Mitigating the Impact of Online Issues:** Offering emotional reassurance can reduce anxiety and promote healing, helping your child process their emotions and move forward.

B) Practical Strategies for Providing Emotional Support

- **Listen Actively and Empathetically:** Give your child your full attention and validate their feelings, showing that you are there to support them.
- **Reassure Them of Their Safety:** Provide comforting words and emphasize your persistent support, reassuring them that they do not have to face the issue alone.
- **Help Them Process Their Emotions:** Encourage open dialogue about their feelings and offer coping strategies, such as deep breathing or engaging in relaxing activities.
- **Be Patient and Supportive:** Understand that emotional recovery takes time, and maintain calm behavior to create a stable environment for your child.
- **Provide Positive Reinforcement:** Praise your child's courage for sharing their concerns and celebrate small victories to boost their confidence and resilience.

C) When Additional Support is Needed

- **Professional Help:** If your child's emotional distress persists, consider seeking professional counselling or therapy to provide additional support.
- **Involving the School or Community Resources:** Contact school counsellors or community support groups to ensure your child receives comprehensive emotional support.

D) Long-Term Emotional Resilience

- **Encouraging Resilience Building:** Help your child recognize their strengths and promote positive thinking by focusing on activities that bring joy and fulfilment.
- **Maintaining Open Communication:** Regularly check in on your child's emotional well-being and reinforce the importance of speaking up about any concerns.

Providing emotional support and reassurance is vital in helping your child navigate the challenges of the online world. By actively listening, offering comfort, and guiding them through their emotions, you play a crucial role in their recovery and long-term well-being. In the next section, we will educate kids on how to take preventive measures to protect against online issues, ensuring their continued safety and security.

9.5 Educating Kids on How to Handle Online Issues

Empowering children with the knowledge and skills to handle online issues is crucial for their safety in the digital world. As they encounter various online challenges, educating them on how to recognize, respond to, and report these issues helps build their confidence and resilience. This section provides strategies for teaching children how to handle online problems effectively.

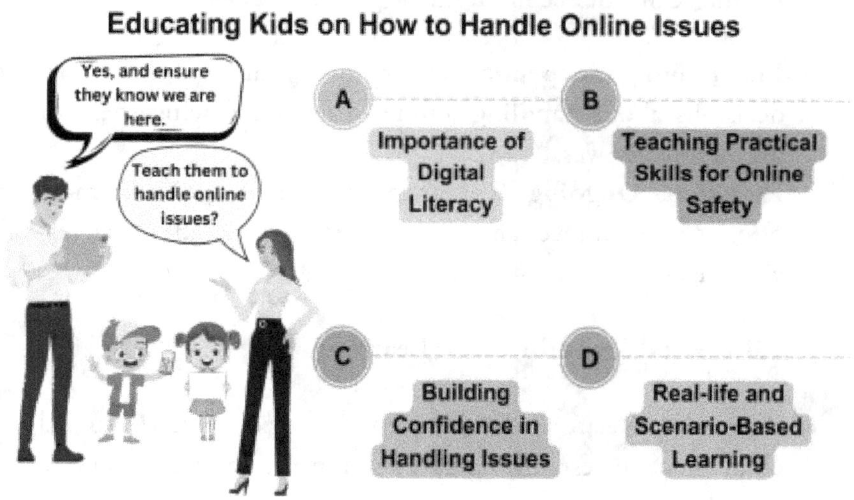

A) The Importance of Digital Literacy

- **Building Awareness:** Educate your child about online risks, such as cyberbullying and privacy breaches, to help them navigate the internet safely.
- **Encouraging Critical Thinking:** Teach them to assess online content critically, recognize bias, and avoid manipulation tactics commonly used by cyberbullies and scammers.

B) Teaching Practical Skills for Online Safety

- **Identifying and Avoiding Threats:** Show your child how to recognize suspicious behavior and use privacy settings to protect their online presence.

- **Responding to Online Issues:** Discuss strategies for handling cyberbullying and unwanted contact, emphasizing the importance of not retaliating and reporting the issue to a trusted adult.
- **Reporting Problems:** Teach your child how and when to report online issues using platform-specific tools and encourage them to document incidents.

C) Building Confidence in Handling Online Issues

- **Encouraging Independence:** Empower your child to make informed decisions about handling online issues, reinforcing their ability to protect themselves.
- **Providing Ongoing Guidance:** Maintain open communication, offering reassurance and support as your child navigates online challenges.

D) Real-life and Scenario-Based Learning

- **Practicing Responses:** Use scenario-based exercises to help your child practice responding to common online issues, building their confidence and preparedness.
- **Learning from Real-Life Examples:** Discuss age-appropriate case studies to illustrate the importance of safe online practices and effective responses.

Educating your child on handling online issues is critical to ensuring their safety in the digital world. By teaching them to recognize risks, respond appropriately, and seek help when needed, you equip them with the tools to navigate the internet confidently. In this chapter, we explored the essential steps parents can take if they suspect online issues affecting their children, from recognizing signs and taking immediate actions to providing emotional support and educating them on how to handle such situations. By staying vigilant and proactive, parents can effectively safeguard their children in the digital world. In the final chapter, we will provide valuable resources for parents to further support and protect their children against these online challenges.

Chapter 10: Resources for Parents

In the ever-evolving digital landscape, safeguarding children's online experiences requires more than just awareness—it demands access to reliable and practical resources. Parents must be equipped with the right tools, knowledge, and support systems to handle the complexities of digital parenting. This chapter is dedicated to providing parents with a comprehensive guide to the most valuable resources available, ensuring that they can protect their children and foster a secure and enriching online environment.

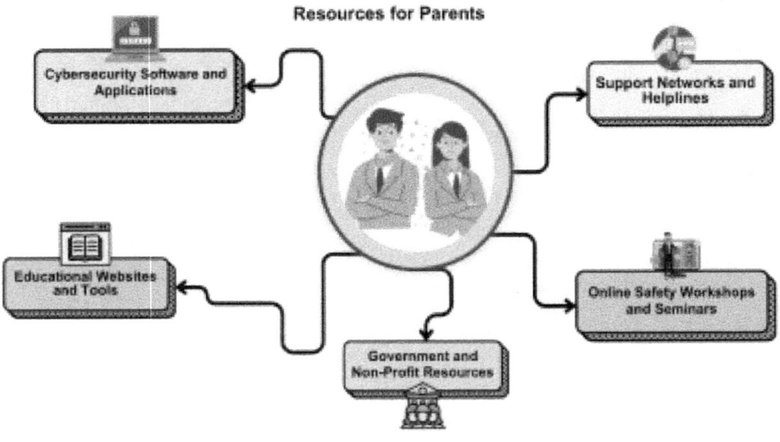

Educational Websites and Tools

Staying informed about the latest trends and threats in the digital world is crucial for effective parenting in the digital age. Educational websites and tools offer a wealth of information, tutorials, and guides that empower parents to understand cybersecurity, online behavior, and digital literacy. These resources break down complex concepts into actionable steps that parents can implement to create a safer online environment for their children.

Cybersecurity Software and Applications

With the rise of cyber threats, having the right cybersecurity tools is essential for protecting your family's digital life. This section will explore some of the most effective cybersecurity software and applications, including antivirus programs, parental control apps, and password managers. These tools help shield your family from risks such as malware, cyberbullying, and privacy breaches, providing peace of mind in the digital world.

Support Networks and Helplines

Dealing with online issues can be challenging, and sometimes parents need additional support. Support networks and helplines offer direct assistance and guidance for families dealing with online challenges. Whether it is cyberbullying, exposure to inappropriate content, or privacy concerns, these networks provide a crucial lifeline, offering expert advice and emotional support when it is needed most.

Online Safety Workshops and Seminars

Education does not stop at home. Online safety workshops and seminars provide parents and children with hands-on learning experiences, equipping them with the skills and knowledge needed to explore the digital world safely. These workshops cover a range of topics, from basic internet safety to advanced cybersecurity practices, ensuring that families are prepared to face online risks with confidence.

Government and Non-Profit Resources

Government agencies and non-profit organizations play a vital role in promoting online safety and providing resources for families. This section will highlight critical resources from these organizations, offering parents access to well-researched, trustworthy information and support. By leveraging these resources, parents can stay informed about best practices, access critical services, and connect with a broader community dedicated to protecting children in the digital age.

In this chapter, we will discuss each of these resources, offering parents a roadmap to creating a secure and supportive digital environment for their children. By utilizing these tools and networks, parents can confidently guide their children through the challenges of the digital world.

10.1 Educational Websites and Tools

When it comes to safeguarding children in the digital world, access to reliable educational resources is crucial. Educational websites and tools provide parents with valuable guidance, tutorials, and information to better understand cybersecurity and digital safety. This section highlights some of the most effective online resources that can help parents create a secure online environment for their children.

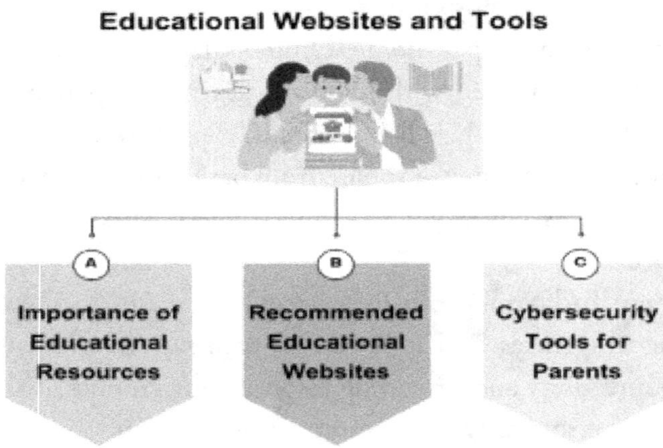

A) The Importance of Educational Resources

- **Staying Updated in a Rapidly Evolving Landscape:** The digital world is constantly changing, with new threats and technologies emerging regularly. Educational websites and tools help parents stay informed about the latest cybersecurity practices, ensuring they can adapt their strategies to protect their children effectively.
- **Empowering Parents with Knowledge:** Many parents may feel overwhelmed by the complexities of cybersecurity. Educational resources break down these concepts into understandable, actionable steps that parents can implement at home, empowering them to take proactive measures to protect their children online.

B) Useful Cybersecurity Tools for Parents

- **Parental Control Apps (e.g., Qustodio, Aura):** Parental control apps help parents monitor their children's online activities, set screen time limits, and block inappropriate content.
- **Password Managers (e.g., LastPass, 1Password):** Password managers ensure all family members use strong, unique passwords across online accounts, storing and auto-filling them securely.
- **Security Software (e.g., Defender, Norton, McAfee):** Most windows devices already comes with free security software called Microsoft Defender. Installing security software on all family devices is essential for protection against malware, viruses, and other online threats.
- **Educational Apps for Kids (e.g., Khan Academy Kids, Code.org):** Educational apps introduce children to technology and cybersecurity concepts in a kid-friendly way.

C) Essential Online Safety Resources Designed for Kids

- **KC7 Cybersecurity game:** The KC7 platform is a non-profit, free online interactive game designed to teach and build practical cybersecurity skills. There is no prior coding or cybersecurity knowledge needed, making it accessible to beginners as young as upper elementary school age.
- **Be Internet Awesome:** This child-focused program teaches kids to be smart, alert, strong, kind, and brave online. Through games and interactive challenges, children learn about password safety, phishing, privacy, cyberbullying, and evaluating online information. It is widely used in schools and homes.
- **Common Sense Media – Kids:** Common Sense Media offers interactive videos, games, quizzes, and lesson plans that teach kids about privacy, cyberbullying, screen time balance, app safety, and respectful online behavior. It also helps children understand how to think critically about what they see online, making it a powerful digital literacy tool.
- **Thinkuknow – Kids & Teens:** Thinkuknow, created by law enforcement and child protection organizations, provides age-specific

safety education for children and teenagers. It includes animated videos, real-life scenarios, classroom-style lessons, and games that teach children how to stay safe from online predators, scams, cyberbullying, and harmful content. It also helps kids learn how to report unsafe behavior with confidence.

- **Childnet – Digital Champions:** Childnet's Digital Champions program encourages children to become leaders in online safety among their peers. It provides kid-friendly guides on topics like protecting personal information, dealing with cyberbullying, understanding online reputation, and practicing kindness online. This resource is especially valuable because it empowers children to help others stay safe too.
- **Internet Matters – For Kids:** Internet Matters offers simple, engaging advice for children about gaming safety, social media use, streaming platforms, screen time, and privacy. The content is designed with visuals, short explanations, and easy language so kids can understand complex digital risks without fear. It also helps children learn what to do if something online makes them uncomfortable.
- **NetSmartz Kids (by the National Center for Missing & Exploited Children):** NetSmartz offers animated videos, games, and lessons that teach kids about online safety, respectful communication, personal boundaries, and what to do if something goes wrong online. It is especially strong in teaching children how to recognize unsafe online interactions.
- **PBS Kids:** PBS Kids integrates online safety lessons into familiar characters and fun educational games. Children learn about kindness online, protecting personal information, being careful what they share, and asking for help when something feels wrong.
- **SafeSurfing with Family Guides:** SafeSurfing provides interactive safety lessons focused on safe downloads, recognizing fake websites, avoiding malware, and understanding how online games and apps can trick users. These guides help children recognize "red flags" such as pop-ups, fake prizes, and suspicious downloads in a very accessible way.

- **StaySafeOnline for Kids (National Cybersecurity Alliance):** This resource teaches children the basics of cybersecurity, such as protecting passwords, avoiding scams, understanding viruses, and practicing safe online habits. It introduces cybersecurity in a simple, non-technical way that builds strong lifelong habits.

10.2 Cybersecurity Software and Applications

In today's connected world, children are exposed to various online threats that can compromise their safety, privacy, and well-being. Parents can deal with these dangers by using reliable cybersecurity software and applications that provide vital protection across digital platforms. This section highlights essential cybersecurity tools that help safeguard against common online threats like cyberbullying, exposure to inappropriate content, and online predators.

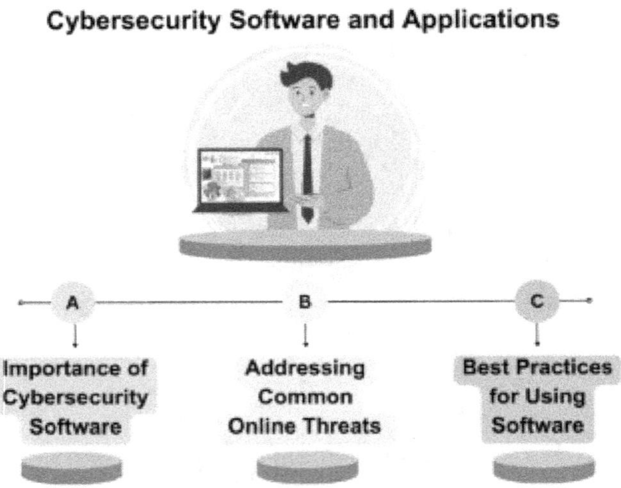

A) The Importance of Cybersecurity Software

- **Comprehensive Protection against Online Threats:** Cybersecurity software acts as the first line of defense, protecting against a range of online threats. With antivirus programs, firewalls, and parental control systems, parents can create a secure digital environment that minimizes risks.
- **Empowering Parents with Control:** These tools not only shield against external threats but also allow parents to monitor and manage their children's online activities, limiting exposure to harmful content and interactions.

B) Addressing Common Online Threats with Cybersecurity Software

1. **Cyberbullying**

- **Recommended Solution**: Bark
- **Key Features:** It monitors texts, emails, and social media for signs of cyberbullying and provides parents with real-time alerts.
- **Benefits:** Enables early intervention, helping parents support their child and stop bullying before it escalates.

1. **Exposure to Inappropriate Content**

- **Recommended Solution:** Net Nanny
- **Key Features:** Advanced content filtering, real-time monitoring, and the ability to block inappropriate websites.
- **Benefits:** Protects children from harmful online content, ensuring a safe digital environment.

1. **Online Predators**

- **Recommended Solution:** Aura
- **Key Features:** Parental controls, location tracking, and monitoring communications across platforms.
- **Benefits:** Detects suspicious behavior early, protecting children from potential predators.

1. **Privacy Risks and Data Security**

- **Recommended Solution:** Norton 360
- **Key Features:** Identity theft protection, secure VPN, and password manager.
- **Benefits:** Safeguards personal information, ensuring that family data remains secure.

1. **Addiction and Overuse**

- **Recommended Solution:** Qustodio
- **Key Features:** Screen time management, daily activity reports, and app blocking.
- **Benefits:** Helps parents control screen time, promoting healthier digital habits.

1. **Phishing and Online Scams**

- **Recommended Solution:** Bitdefender Total Security
- **Key Features:** Anti-phishing protection and real-time threat detection.
- **Benefits:** Protects children from phishing scams by blocking fraudulent activities.

1. **Malware and Viruses**

- **Recommended Solution:** McAfee Total Protection
- **Key Features:** Antivirus protection, anti-malware, and firewall capabilities.
- **Benefits:** Protects devices from malware and viruses, maintaining a secure digital environment.

C) Best Practices for Using Cybersecurity Software

- **Regularly Update Software:** Keep all cybersecurity software up-to-date to protect against the latest threats.
- **Customize Settings for Your Child's Needs:** For adequate protection, customize the settings to match your child's online activities and maturity level.
- **Monitor and Review Regularly:** Review the reports and alerts generated regularly to stay informed about your child's online activities.
- **Educate Your Child:** Teach your child about online safety and how to recognize potential threats.

Cybersecurity software and applications are essential tools for protecting children from online threats. From preventing cyberbullying to safeguarding against malware, these tools provide comprehensive protection, ensuring your child can safely explore the digital world.

10.3 Support Networks and Helplines

In addition to cybersecurity tools and educational resources, support networks and helplines are vital for parents managing their children's online safety. These services offer guidance, emotional support, and expert advice when dealing with issues such as cyberbullying, exposure to harmful content, and interactions with online predators. This section highlights the importance of these resources and provides recommendations for support networks and helplines that can assist parents in protecting their children's well-being in the digital world.

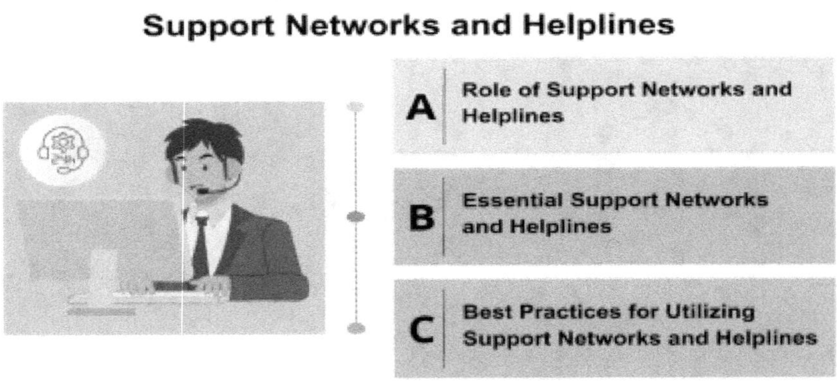

A) The Role of Support Networks and Helplines

- **Providing Expert Advice and Guidance:** Support networks and helplines connect parents with experts who offer tailored advice on specific online challenges. Whether dealing with cyberbullying or seeking general guidance on internet safety, these resources help parents make informed decisions.
- **Offering Emotional Support:** Navigating online issues can be stressful for both parents and children. Support networks provide a community where parents can share experiences, receive empathy, and gain encouragement from others who understand the challenges of digital parenting.
- **Facilitating Timely Interventions**: In urgent situations—such as

encounters with online predators or severe cyberbullying—helplines offer quick, actionable advice, guiding parents through the necessary steps to protect their child and report the issue.

B) Essential Support Networks and Helplines for Parents

- **National Center for Missing & Exploited Children (NCMEC) - CyberTipline:** The CyberTipline is a national helpline for reporting child exploitation, online predators, and other severe online threats. It offers 24/7 support and connects parents with law enforcement.
- **Childnet International - Parent Resources and Helpline:** Childnet International provides a helpline offering advice on issues like cyberbullying, online privacy, and inappropriate content, along with a wealth of online resources for parents.
- **The National Bullying Prevention Center (PACER)—Parent Helpline**: PACER's helpline offers support for parents dealing with bullying, including cyberbullying, and provides strategies for prevention and intervention.
- **Internet Matters - Parent Support Services:** Internet Matters offers a helpline and a comprehensive website with resources on digital parenting, including managing online risks and setting up parental controls.
- **StopBullying.gov - Online Bullying Resources:** StopBullying.gov provides extensive resources for understanding and combating bullying, with a focus on both prevention and intervention.

C) Best Practices for Utilizing Support Networks and Helplines

- **Reach out Early:** Be sure to seek help before a problem escalates. Early intervention can prevent issues from worsening and provide your child with the support they need to deal with online challenges safely.
- **Keep Communication Open:** Maintain open lines of communication with your child and involve them in discussions about seeking help. This approach builds trust and helps your child feel more

comfortable reaching out for support.

- **Combine Resources:** Use support networks and helplines alongside cybersecurity tools and educational resources. This comprehensive approach ensures you address both the technical and emotional aspects of your child's online safety.
- **Document and Report:** If your child is experiencing severe online issues, document all relevant information and share it with the helpline or support network. Proper documentation is crucial for effective intervention and resolution.

Support networks and helplines are essential resources for parents managing and resolving online safety challenges. Whether you need expert advice, emotional support, or immediate assistance, these services are invaluable for ensuring your child's safety and well-being in the digital world.

10.4 Online Safety Workshops and Seminars

Attending online safety workshops and seminars is an empowering resource for parents. It equips them with the knowledge and skills to confidently explore the digital world and protect their children. Led by experts in cybersecurity and child psychology, these events provide practical strategies for online safety. This section explores the benefits of participating in such workshops, recommends reputable options, and offers tips on maximizing their value.

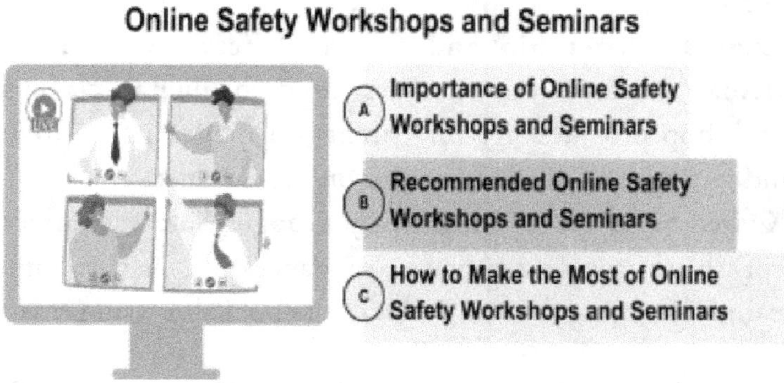

A) The Importance of Online Safety Workshops and Seminars

- **Staying Updated on Emerging Threats:** The digital landscape is constantly evolving. Workshops and seminars offer parents the latest information on online threats, ensuring they are equipped to address current and future challenges.
- **Learning from Experts:** These events are hosted by professionals specializing in online safety, providing parents with credible, research-based information and practical advice.
- **Networking with Other Parents:** Workshops also offer opportunities to connect with other parents facing similar challenges, promoting a supportive community and sharing solutions for managing online safety.

B) Recommended Online Safety Workshops and Seminars

- **"Keeping Kids Safe Online" by the National Cyber Security Alliance (NCSA):** This workshop covers a wide range of topics, including privacy settings, social media safety, and cyberbullying prevention. The expert-led sessions are interactive, providing parents with personalized advice and access to additional resources.
- **"Parenting in a Digital World" by Cyber Safe Kids:** This seminar helps parents deal with digital parenting challenges by offering strategies for screen time management, cyberbullying, and online privacy. The seminar is practical, with real-world examples and case studies.
- **"Digital Citizenship and Online Safety" by Common Sense Media:** Focused on teaching children digital citizenship, this workshop provides tips for parents on modelling positive behavior and setting clear expectations for online conduct.
- **"Cyber Safety for Families" by Google Safety Center**: Google's workshops provide step-by-step guidance on using their built-in safety features, securing devices, and setting up safe browsing environments.

C) How to Make the Most of Online Safety Workshops and Seminars

- **Prepare in Advance:** Identify specific online safety challenges your family faces and prepare questions to focus on relevant parts of the event.
- **Engage Actively:** Participate by asking questions, taking notes, engaging with presenters and attendees, and seeking advice about your family's situation.
- **Follow Up with Action:** After the workshop, implement strategies and tools immediately, such as adjusting privacy settings or setting new screen time rules.
- **Stay Connected**: Utilize additional resources or join communities offered by the workshops to deepen your understanding and maintain a support network.

Online safety workshops and seminars are valuable for parents who want to enhance their knowledge and skills in protecting their children online. By participating in these events, parents can stay informed, learn from experts, and connect with other parents facing similar challenges.

10.5 Government and Non-Profit Resources

Government agencies and non-profit organizations offer crucial resources for parents aiming to protect their children's digital lives. These resources range from educational materials to direct support, helping parents deal with online challenges effectively. This section highlights vital resources from government and non-profit entities that provide trustworthy guidance, support services, and community connections for families.

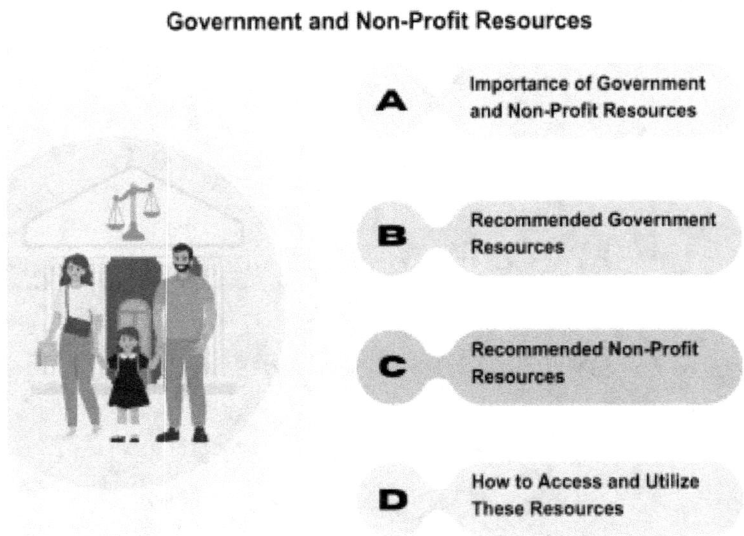

A) The Importance of Government and Non-Profit Resources

- **Reliable Information and Guidance:** Government and non-profit organizations provide expert-driven, well-researched information on online safety, ensuring parents receive accurate and current advice.
- **Support for Families:** Many of these organizations offer direct support, such as helplines and counselling, to help families address complex online issues like cyberbullying or privacy breaches.
- **Advocacy and Awareness:** Non-profits play a vital role in promoting safer online environments and raising awareness of digital risks, offering parents a platform to engage in broader protective efforts.

B) Recommended Government Resources

- **Federal Trade Commission (FTC) – Online Safety:** The FTC provides comprehensive resources on online safety, including guides on protecting personal information and avoiding scams. These resources are ideal for understanding legal aspects and taking proactive steps to secure children's online experiences.
- **Department of Education – Digital Citizenship:** Offers resources to help parents teach digital citizenship, focusing on critical thinking and responsible online behavior. These materials are perfect for instilling strong digital values in children.
- **Federal Bureau of Investigation (FBI) – Safe Online Surfing:** The FBI's Safe Online Surfing program provides age-appropriate lessons on online safety for students, making learning about digital security fun and accessible.

C) Recommended Non-Profit Resources

- **Family Online Safety Institute (FOSI):** FOSI provides a wealth of resources focused on making the online world safer for kids and families. They offer practical tools, research, and tips to help parents manage their children's technology use effectively.
- **National Center for Missing & Exploited Children (NCMEC):** NCMEC provides resources for preventing online exploitation, including reporting tools and support services. It is essential for parents concerned about online safety and exploitation risks.
- **Internet Watch Foundation (IWF):** Focused on eliminating online child sexual abuse content, the IWF offers reporting tools and resources to help parents protect their children from online exploitation.

D) How to Access and Utilize These Resources

- **Explore Available Materials:** Visit the websites of these organizations to access guides, toolkits, and educational programs that align with your family's needs.

- **Incorporate Resources into Daily Life:** Use these tools and information in your daily parenting practices to strengthen your child's online safety.
- **Stay Connected and Informed:** Subscribe to newsletters and participate in webinars offered by these organizations to stay updated on the latest online safety developments.

Government and non-profit resources are essential for protecting children in the digital world. By utilizing these materials and support services, parents can enhance their efforts to safeguard their children's online experiences, ensuring a safer and more secure digital environment for their families. The resources provided by government agencies and non-profit organizations are invaluable tools for parents committed to protecting their children in the digital age. By leveraging these trusted sources of information, support, and community, parents can confidently navigate the complexities of online safety, ensuring a secure and positive digital environment for their families. As we conclude this chapter, remember that staying informed and proactive is critical to safeguarding your child's online experiences.

Concluding the Journey: Protecting Our Kids Online

As we reach the end of this guide, it is clear that the digital world presents both incredible opportunities and significant challenges for our children. The internet offers a wealth of knowledge, creativity, and connectivity, but it also exposes young users to risks that can impact their safety, well-being, and development. As parents, your role in guiding children through these issues is more critical than ever, underscoring your value and significance in your children's lives.

Throughout this book, we have explored the various aspects of digital parenting, from understanding your children's online activities to implementing vital security measures and from encouraging open communication to actively participating in their digital lives. The strategies, tools, and resources provided are designed to equip you with the knowledge and confidence needed to create a secure and enriching online environment for your children, empowering you as a parent.

One of the primary ideas is the importance of education—both for you and your children. Staying informed about the latest trends in cybersecurity and digital behavior is essential in adapting to the ever-evolving digital world. Equally important is teaching your children about the realities of the internet, empowering them with the skills and knowledge to make safe and responsible choices online.

The role of emotional support cannot be pointed out. As children encounter various challenges online, from cyberbullying to exposure to inappropriate content, your guidance and reassurance are vital in helping them deal with these experiences and emerge stronger. Building a foundation of trust and open communication ensures that your children feel comfortable coming to you with their concerns, allowing you to provide the necessary support and intervention when needed.

Moreover, the resources available—whether through educational websites, cybersecurity software, or support networks—enable you to take proactive measures in safeguarding your child's digital life. These tools and resources are there to support you, providing expert guidance, practical advice, and a community of parents facing similar challenges, ensuring you are not alone on this journey.

As you continue this journey, remember that digital parenting is an ongoing process. The strategies and practices outlined in this book are not one-time solutions but part of a continuous effort to adapt, learn, and grow alongside your children as they explore the digital world. By remaining engaged, informed, and supportive, you are not only protecting your children today but also empowering them to become responsible, confident digital citizens in the future.

In closing, your devotion to ensuring your child's digital future demonstrates your love and dedication as a parent. By taking these precautions, you are not only safeguarding your children from potential dangers but also preparing them for a future in which they may securely use technology to study, create, and connect with the world around them. Together, we can create a safer digital environment for future generations.

www.ingramcontent.com/pod-product-compliance
Lightning Source LLC
LaVergne TN
LVHW052304200926
848481LV00002B/461